RAND NATIONAL DEFENSE RESEARCH INSTITUTE

Small Business and Strategic Sourcing

Lessons from Past Research and Current Data

Nancy Y. Moore, Clifford A. Grammich, Judith D. Mele

Prepared for the Office of the Secretary of Defense

For more information on this publication, visit www.rand.org/t/rr410

Library of Congress Cataloging-in-Publication Data
ISBN: 978-0-8330-8230-5

Published by the RAND Corporation, Santa Monica, Calif.
© Copyright 2014 RAND Corporation
RAND® is a registered trademark.

Support RAND
Make a tax-deductible charitable contribution at
www.rand.org/giving/contribute

www.rand.org

Preface

In addition to its paramount goal of meeting warfighter requirements, the Department of Defense (DoD) has a number of goals to fulfill in its procurement of goods and services. These other policy goals include meeting small-business goals, in which approximately 23 percent of its prime-contract dollars for goods and services are to be spent with small businesses, saving on procurement, and, ultimately, making the most effective use of taxpayer dollars. Depending on how they are approached, some of these goals can conflict with one another. Some best purchasing practices, for example, recommend consolidation of requirements and rationalization of the supply base, in which purchasers may devise fewer, larger, longer-term contracts with fewer, and often larger, suppliers to reduce total costs.

This document explores the challenges DoD may face in applying strategic-sourcing practices to make its purchasing more effective and efficient in ways that will not conflict with meeting its small-business goals. It draws from a wide variety of RAND research on both strategic sourcing and small-business policies. It also explores how future DoD budgets will likely change in their mix of spending and the opportunities for strategic sourcing and small-business contracting. It identifies industries where increasing small-business contracting may be feasible, and it leverages previous RAND work on both strategic sourcing and small-business policies with updated analyses of possible trends in future DoD expenditures and their implications for small-business contracting.

This document should be of general interest to policymakers concerned with procurement and small-business policy and of specific interest to small-business offices within DoD and the military services, the Small Business Administration, and members of Congress concerned with military procurement and small-business issues.

This research was conducted within the Acquisition and Technology Policy Center of the RAND National Defense Research Institute, a federally funded research and development center sponsored by the Office of the Secretary of Defense, the Joint Staff, the Unified Combatant Commands, the Navy, the Marine Corps, the defense agencies, and the defense Intelligence Community.

For more information on the Acquisition and Technology Policy Center, see http://www.rand.org/nsrd/ndri/centers/atp.html or contact the director (contact information is provided on the web page).

Contents

Figures

Tables

Summary

The Department of Defense (DoD) must meet a variety of goals in purchasing more than $350 billion in goods and services every year. Above all, of course, it must meet the paramount goal of fulfilling warfighter requirements but, in doing so, it has other statutory and policy goals to meet as well. One goal is to spend approximately 23 percent of its prime-contract dollars for goods and services with firms identified as small within their industry. More recently, DoD has also pursued strategic-sourcing goals through the use of best buying practices as is common practice within leading enterprises.

This document explores the challenges DoD might face in implementing strategic-sourcing practices in ways that will not conflict with its small-business contracting goals while making its purchasing more effective and efficient. Small-business goals, which can involve larger numbers of suppliers, may be in tension with strategic-sourcing goals that favor fewer suppliers. In drawing from the wide variety of RAND research on related topics, we summarize the development of small-business procurement policies and their application to DoD, research on strategic-sourcing practices, and what both mean for likely future budgetary trends in DoD.

DoD Purchases from Small Business over Time

In recent years, DoD has spent between 20 and 25 percent of its prime-contract dollars for goods and services from small businesses (Figure S.1). Although the government-wide goal is currently 23 percent (with the Small Business Administration working with individual agencies to set goals for each), Congress has considered legislation to increase it to 25 percent or higher.

Complicating the challenge of meeting small-business goals is the adoption of proven business practices for reducing total costs. More strategic sourcing may lead to consolidation of supply requirements and, hence, increased use of larger businesses over smaller ones.

Changing mixes of purchases can also affect the use of suppliers. When Congress last increased the small-business goal in 1997, DoD spending, in constant dollars, was near its lowest point of the past half-century. Perhaps more important, DoD spending on weapon system procurement was also at its lowest point of the past half-century. The mix of its purchases matters for DoD's ability to meet small-business contracting goals. And, among the many industries that supply weapon systems, DoD has historically spent little with small businesses.

DoD has spent more with small businesses outside weapons-related industries, such as those providing fighter aircraft, tanks, and submarines. For example, it spends nearly all its

Figure S.1
DoD Expenditures and Small-Business Utilization

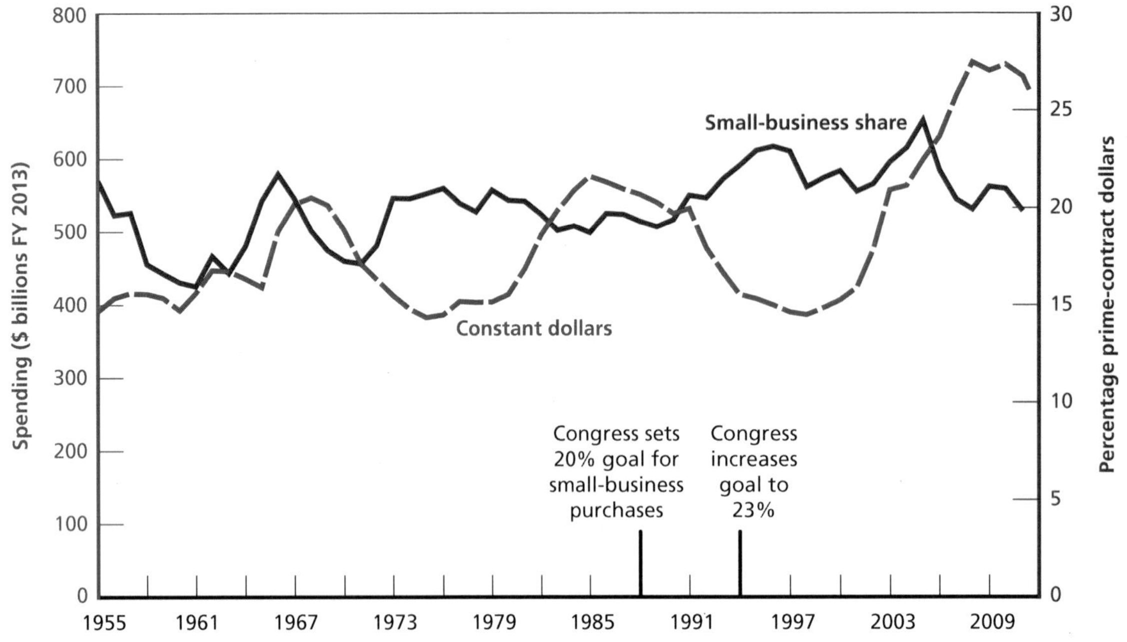

SOURCES: Foreman (2008); DoD Office of Small Business Programs (undated).
RAND RR410-S.1

money for janitorial services and landscaping services with small businesses and tradition-ally has spent more with small businesses in appropriation categories, such as Operations and Maintenance (O&M), Military Construction, and Family Housing than it has for areas such as weapon system procurement. The problem with small-business utilization is that DoD spending on O&M has decreased even more than total DoD spending (Figure S.2). That for military construction and family housing, already very small, has also decreased. Put another way, the mix of DoD expenditures may have become more unfavorable for small businesses.

Existing Opportunities for Strategic Sourcing and Their Implications for Small-Business Utilization

To be sure, there are ways to implement strategic-sourcing practices that support small businesses. These may include consolidating contracts with small businesses, particularly across purchase offices or categories of goods and services.

For example, as ranked by number of contracts, ten contractors have more than 1,350 contracts written and used by DoD, with two contractors each having more than 2,000 such contracts.[1] Three of these ten are small businesses. One, Kampi Components Co., Inc., has

---

[1]   In this document, we analyze contracts both written and used by DoD. The distinction is important because DoD is best able to influence purchasing practices over contracts it both writes and uses, rather than those of another agency, such as the General Services Agency, it may use to purchase goods and services.

Figure S.2
DoD Spending, by Category, Recent and Projected, Fiscal Year (FY) 2006 to FY 2018

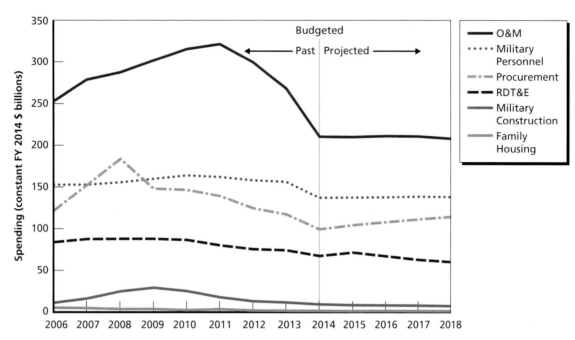

SOURCE: Office of the Under Secretary of Defense (Comptroller) (2013).
RAND *RR410-S.2*

more than 2,600 contracts. Consolidating requirements fulfilled by Kampi could reduce the number of DoD's contracts with Kampi, thereby increasing DoD's leverage over the company and also reducing its workload as well as that for contracting offices while having little effect on DoD fulfillment of small-business goals.

Multiple contracts for the same commodity may also offer some strategic-sourcing opportunities through contract consolidation. DoD has at least 4,200 contracts for goods and services in ten Product and Service Codes (PSCs). For all of these, the number of contracts exceeds the number of contractors. This indicates that there may be some opportunity for consolidation of purchases of similar goods and services from the same supplier. For five of these PSCs, DoD spent more than 50 percent with small businesses. Across all purchases, DoD had a number of contracts that was nearly seven times the number of contractors. For automatic data processing software, for example, DoD has more than 7,000 contracts with fewer than 2,500 suppliers, nearly half of which are small businesses. Consolidating contracts with some small businesses selling these goods, or otherwise establishing opportunities for preferred small-business suppliers, might offer some opportunities for strategic-sourcing initiatives. At the same time, other ways will have to be found to meet strategic-sourcing goals, given the relatively small amount of money DoD spends for these particular goods.

Having multiple purchasers of the same commodity may offer still further strategic-sourcing opportunities. More than 340 purchase offices buy goods and services from each of ten different PSCs, indicating how widely used these goods and services are. Nevertheless, there may be opportunities for contract consolidation and strategic sourcing across these multiple purchase offices. For all the PSCs of common goods and services, the number of contracts is at least three times the number of purchase offices buying such goods and services. This likely indicates that purchase offices are using multiple contracts to buy similar goods and services. The number of contracts also exceeds the number of suppliers. Many of the purchases for these common items acquired across purchase offices are with small businesses; in five of these PSCs, DoD spent at least 40 percent of its dollars with small businesses. For example, nearly 500 purchase offices have more than 2,300 contracts to purchase office furniture from fewer than 1,000 firms, more than two-fifths of which are small businesses. Establishing some preferred small-business suppliers and consolidating contracts with them, up to the small-business size threshold established for their industries, could help meet strategic-sourcing goals and reduce demands on contract staff.

Identifying industries where DoD spends a large amount of money and has a large number of contracts used by a large number of purchase offices offers another way to identify strategic-sourcing opportunities. Altogether, 14 industries rank among the top 50 for receiving DoD dollars, for number of DoD contracts, and for number of purchase offices buying goods and services in the industry. Yet, DoD small-business purchases remain quite infrequent in several of these. There may be valid reasons why small-business utilization is low in some industries. These may include concentration and consolidation within certain industries, which, in turn, presumably, lead to an increase in the minimum size an individual firm needs to be to compete in such industries. In the 14 industries receiving large numbers of DoD dollars and contracts, a small proportion of large firms (having at least 5,000 employees or more than $100 million in annual receipts) are responsible for much larger proportions of industry activity.

Reconsidering Industry Thresholds

For many industries in which DoD purchases goods and services, the small business share in the federal marketplace differs from that in the overall industry. Although there may be many reasons for this, industry-size standards contribute to the disparity. Industries classified by size can be very varied, including many activities of little importance to DoD and likely undertaken by smaller firms than those with which it can effectively contract.

Changing economic conditions over time have also affected size thresholds. There is some evidence that economic activity is more concentrated among larger firms than in the past. Yet, for most manufacturing industries, the size threshold remains at 500 employees, and receipts-based thresholds have not always kept pace with inflation. Data issues also indicate some problems with current thresholds and their effectiveness in identifying small business.

Such issues matter for strategic sourcing because, although the federal government has long sought to boost small business, in setting small-business procurement preferences it has also sought to boost businesses of sufficient size to handle federal contracting. To better identify small businesses that can both meet competitiveness goals and support strategic-sourcing efforts, policymakers may wish to reconsider some criteria used to set small-business size thresholds.

In particular, the size threshold for a small business might be based in part on the minimum size required to be an ongoing concern in a particular industry. The Small Business Administration (SBA) could review production processes in an industry to determine the minimum firm size needed to remain competitive. Data on establishment births, deaths, expansions, and contractions by industrial sectors, as available in the Statistics of U.S. Businesses, may also be informative. The size needed to remain competitive may be greater than that of firms entering an industry, because new firms may expect to lose money during a startup period. Access to credit on favorable terms is also critical to a firm's ability to enter the market, finance ongoing operations, and expand. SBA could therefore base an industry's size threshold in part on the firm size needed to access credit on reasonable terms. For procurement purposes, policymakers may also wish to ensure that the small-business size threshold is sufficient not just to compete for and administer federal prime contracts but also to support the administrative and reporting requirements of such contracts.

Small-business size thresholds should also consider industry characteristics, including the distribution of firms in concentrated industries. Such criteria could further promote competitiveness. They might include industry-concentration indices.

Using multiple criteria to determine what is a "small" business will require a weighting scheme. Regardless of which criteria are chosen and how they are weighted, policymakers should ensure that the resulting size threshold is the largest indicated by all criteria adopted and not an average of the standards.

Improved and more precise industry definitions might help to set small-business size thresholds for government purposes—and to identify small businesses that can both help boost competitiveness and be of sufficient size to help DoD meet its strategic-sourcing goals. This could include determining if industries are defined properly for purposes of setting small-business size thresholds and how firm activity in an industry might best be measured. Conditions in some industries may change over time, necessitating a differing measure or threshold. Regardless of how firm size is measured, any method should consider the minimum firm size needed to stay competitive and perform government work, weighing as necessary those characteristics most appropriate for government preferences.

Adjusting to Changing DoD Needs

In coming years, we expect that DoD budget cuts will change its mix of spending, which is linked to its small-business contracting and strategic-sourcing opportunities. In particular, we expect that DoD will cut its O&M spending and its spending in the industries associated with it. Because DoD already spends a large proportion of its dollars with small businesses providing such goods and services, it will have to either increase its small-business spending in these areas still further, or find other areas in which to increase it to meet its small-business contracting goals.

More generally, to meet its future small-business contracting goals, DoD may need to press to revise industry

- thresholds to reflect not only inflation but also industry consolidation
- metrics, such as high inputs to production, to reflect the realities of certain industry operations
- definitions to reflect the demographics of industries as well as new and emerging technologies that do not fit the current definitions.

Strategic sourcing could benefit some small firms by providing them with fewer, larger, longer-term contracts. Yet such opportunities are limited by current industry definitions and SBA size policies.

To ensure that its goals for small-business utilization and strategic sourcing do not conflict, we recommend that DoD identify the industries where it has opportunities to increase its small-business utilization rate through strategic sourcing. We further recommend that DoD consider developing a small-business preferred-supplier program for those small businesses that have demonstrated good performance and value.

DoD may wish to strongly advocate raising small-business thresholds where industries are highly consolidated or are consolidating, as well as where thresholds have not kept pace with inflation. It may also wish to work with policymakers to improve and expedite SBA's process for determining thresholds and to validate or change industry metrics that do not adequately reflect the realities of doing business. Finally, it may want to work with the Office of Management and Budget to redefine industry definitions to better reflect industry demographics as well as emerging technologies.

In pursuing both strategic sourcing and small-business initiatives, DoD will continually face tensions between the two. Small-business goals seek, in part, to increase the number of firms participating in federal government contracts. Strategic sourcing, by contrast would lead to more requirements being met by fewer firms, with small firms receiving larger contracts increasingly at risk of exceeding the size threshold for their industry. Given the charge to pursue both small-business policies and strategic-sourcing initiatives, DoD policymakers may understandably seek to apply strategic sourcing to their contracts with small businesses as well as with other-than-small businesses. This document shows some ways that they can do so. Yet the tension between the two goals will remain.

Acknowledgments

In large part, this work summarizes several relevant RAND reports published over the years. In addition to thanking the authors of those works (cited in our references), we thank Amy Cox, Mary Chenoweth, and Aaron Kofner in helping update their research for this document. We also acknowledge previously unpublished work of Lloyd Dixon that we have adapted for this publication. We are also grateful to Tim Bonds and Ken Girardini for their support of a small internal project that formed the foundation of portions of this report, as well as to Cynthia Cook and Irv Blickstein for their support of this effort. William Shelton and Mary Chenoweth provided several excellent suggestions in their reviews of this work that helped strengthen our presentation. Finally, we thank Donna Mead for her help in preparing this document for publication and our reviewers, William Shelton and Mary Chenoweth, for their insights and comments.

Abbreviations

ADP	automatic data processing
CCR	Central Contractor Registry
CFR	Code of Federal Regulations
DoD	Department of Defense
FPDS	Federal Procurement Data System
FY	fiscal year
HHI	Herfindahl-Hirshman Index
LLC	limited-liability company
NAICS	North American Industry Classification System
O&M	operations and maintenance
PSC	Product and Service Code
RDT&E	research, development, test, and evaluation
RFC	Reconstruction Finance Corporation
SBA	Small Business Administration
SDPA	Small Defense Plants Administration
SIC	Standard Industrial Classification
SWPC	Smaller War Plants Corporation
TAS	Treasury Account Symbol

CHAPTER ONE

The Intersection of Small-Business Policies and Strategic-Sourcing Practices

Department of Defense as a Purchaser

The Department of Defense (DoD) is among the world's largest purchasers of goods and services (Czech and Mueller, 2011). Approximately two-thirds of its budget in fiscal year (FY) 2012—a proportion that has grown over time—was for nonpersonnel expenditures. In addition to weapon systems, DoD purchases include such varied products as engineering services, food, clothing, landscaping services, and many others from more than 1,000 industries (as defined by six-digit codes of the North American Industry Classification System, or NAICS).

The more than $350 billion DoD spends annually for goods and services attracts policymakers' attention not only for its size but also for its effect on the economy and the government budget. Lawmakers, as part of their efforts to preserve free competitive enterprise and to strengthen the overall economy of the nation (see Public Law 85-536, as amended January 3, 2013), have sought to provide the maximum practicable opportunity for small businesses to participate in providing goods and services to the government. At the same time, given a need to accomplish more with less, DoD officials are seeking a variety of savings when purchasing goods and services, including through use of best business buying practices that may not always be compatible with small-business goals for prime-contract spending.

Over time, RAND researchers have conducted pioneering work for DoD and the military services on both best practices in purchasing and supply management and small-business policies. Their work on purchasing and supply management has included research on spend analyses, strategic sourcing, market research, supply-strategy development, supplier-relationship management, and supply-chain risk management (see, for example, Moore et al., 2004; Chenoweth and Grammich, 2006; Moore et al., 2007; Moore et al., 2011; Saunders et al., 1995; Hanks et al., 2005; Nicosia and Moore, 2006; Moore, Grammich, and Bickel, 2007; Chenoweth, Arkes, and Moore, 2010; Moore, Cox, et al., 2012; Chenoweth et al., 2012; and Moore and Loredo, 2013). Their work on small-business policies has included historical analyses of small business and defense acquisitions, assessment of methods for setting small-business size standards, ways to enhance small-business opportunities in DoD, and identifying and removing barriers to successful contracting (see, for example, Grammich et al., 2011; Gu, Karoly, and Zissimopoulos, 2010; Gates and Leuschner, eds., 2007; Moore et al., 2008; and Cox, Moore, and Grammich, forthcoming). RAND researchers have also done work on such related topics as industrial-base issues, best practices for procurement organization and staffing, contracting workforce and workload, operational contract support, and leading successful change (see, for example, Birkler et al., 2011; Schank et al., 2011; Moore, Cox, et al., 2012; and Moore, Wang, et al., 2012).

This document explores the challenges DoD may face in applying strategic-sourcing practices in ways that will not conflict with its small-business contracting goals but that do make its purchasing more effective and efficient. In drawing from the wide variety of RAND research on related topics, we summarize the development of small-business procurement policies and their application to DoD, research on strategic-sourcing practices, and what both mean for likely future budgetary trends in DoD. We begin with a broad overview of DoD spending.

Trends in DoD Spending

DoD spending over time has largely been cyclical (Figure 1.1). Peaks coincided roughly with the Korean War, the Vietnam War, the 1980s Cold War buildup, and the wars in Afghanistan and Iraq in the past decade. The proposed DoD budget for FY 2014, $528 billion, is a decrease of 24 percent in nominal dollars from the FY 2010 budget and of 29 percent in constant dollars. Although out-year projections show a modest increase in nominal dollars, they show a modest decrease in constant dollars.[1]

Figure 1.1
DoD Budget in Nominal and Constant (FY 2014) Dollars, Actual and Projected, FY 1948 to FY 2018

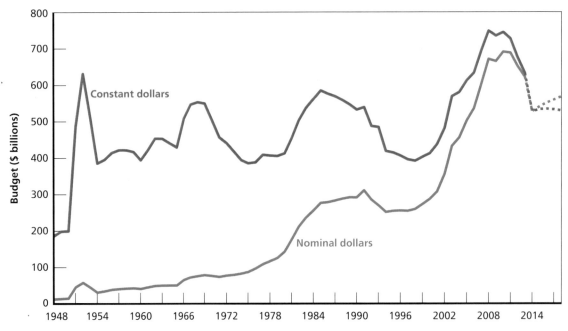

SOURCE: Office of the Under Secretary of Defense (Comptroller) (2013).
RAND *RR410-1.1*

---

[1]   This discussion should be considered illustrative more than predictive. Budget "sequestration" could reduce defense budgets for future years by 10 percent or more (Freedberg, 2013). Our budget projections do not include supplemental funds or those for overseas contingency operations, both of which will likely be included in upcoming budgets.

Although total DoD spending has fluctuated over time, the proportion spent on purchasing goods and services (or all DoD expenditures except personnel) has risen somewhat steadily. Nonpersonnel expenditures for DoD comprise three main types: weapon-system procurement; research, development, test, and evaluation (RDT&E); and other goods and services. Altogether, such expenditures now represent more than two-thirds of the DoD budget (Figure 1.2). The greatest growth in these purchases has been for other goods and services. Whereas such purchases accounted for about one-tenth of the DoD budget through the mid-1960s, today they account for more than one-third.

When contracting for many of these purchases, DoD has a number of goals to meet. Among these are the congressional goal that 23 percent of all federal government prime-contract dollars be awarded to small businesses. Over the years, DoD's support of small businesses has varied between a low of 16 percent and a high of 25 percent (Figure 1.3).[2] Given that DoD prime-contract dollars account for about two-thirds of all federal government prime-contract dollars, how well DoD does in supporting small businesses greatly affects the ability of the entire federal government to meet the congressional goal.[3]

Figure 1.2
Procurement of Goods and Services Has Accounted for Two-Thirds of Recent DoD Budgets

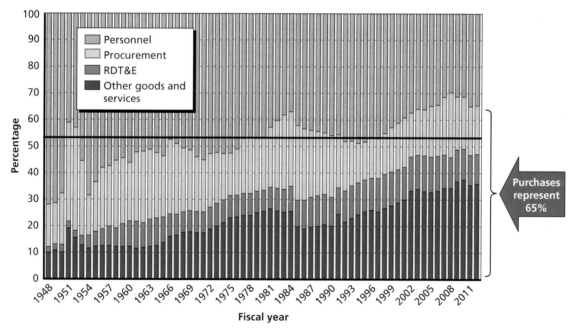

SOURCE: Office of the Under Secretary of Defense (Comptroller) (2013).
RAND *RR410-1.2*

---

[2]   Small-business purchases in recent years are shown as a percentage of goaling dollars, a subset of prime-contract dollars that we will discuss in more depth in Chapter Three.

[3]   The Small Business Administration (SBA) works with each federal agency to set an agency-specific goal that will help the federal government meet the government-wide goal of 23.0 percent. For FY 2013, these goals ranged from 10.0 percent for the Department of Energy to 67.0 percent for SBA. The DoD goal for FY 2013 was 22.5 percent; in recent years, it has ranged from 22.24 to 23.0 percent. We surmise that, given the large portion of federal purchases made by DoD, its agency-specific goal cannot vary far from the statutory government-wide goal of 23.0 percent. For more on the process for setting agency-specific goals, see SBA (undated-a).

Figure 1.3
DoD Expenditures and Small-Business Utilization

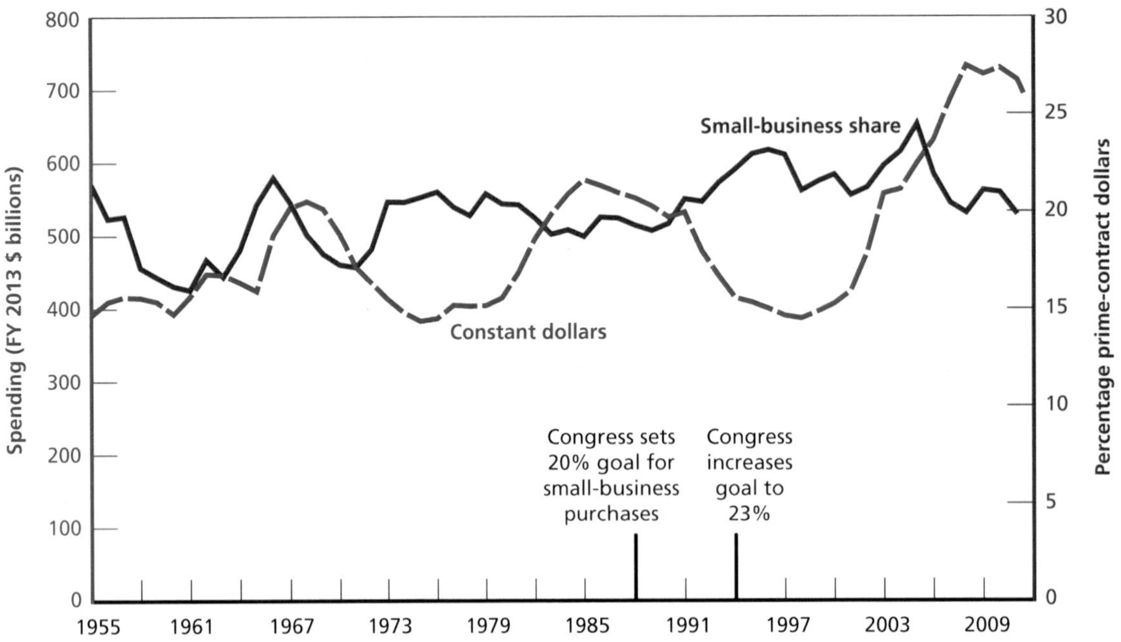

SOURCES: Foreman (2008); Office of Small Business Programs (undated-b).
RAND *RR410-1.3*

Congress has both increased the small-business goal and added specific categories of small-business subgoals over time. It set the overall small-business procurement goal at 20 percent in 1988, increased it to 23 percent in 1997, and, in 2013, was considering legislation that would increase it to 25 percent or more (Grammich et al., 2011; Manuel and Lunder, 2013). In addition, Congress has set subgoals for small businesses that are owned by women, service-disabled veterans, "disadvantaged" persons, or those with a principal office and at least 35 percent of their employees residing in a designated Historically Underutilized Business Zone (also known as HUBZones).

Challenges Facing DoD in Meeting Small-Business Contracting Goals

When Congress last increased the small-business contracting goal in 1997, DoD spending, in constant dollars, was near its lowest point of the past half-century. Perhaps more important, DoD spending on weapon-system procurement was also at its lowest point of the past half-century. The mix of its purchases matters for DoD's ability to meet small-business goals. And, for many industries that supply weapon systems (e.g., aircraft manufacturing, military armored vehicle manufacturing, ship building), DoD has historically spent little with small businesses (Moore et al., 2008).

DoD has spent more with small businesses outside weapons-related industries, such as those providing fighter aircraft, tanks, and submarines. For example, it spends nearly all its money for janitorial services and landscaping services with small businesses and traditionally has spent more with small businesses in such DoD budget categories as Operations and

Maintenance (O&M), Military Construction, and Family Housing than it has in such areas as weapon-system procurement (Moore et al., 2008). The problem for small-business procurement is that DoD spending on O&M has decreased even more than total DoD expenditures in recent years (Office of the Under Secretary of Defense [Comptroller], 2013). Spending on Military Construction and Family Housing, which is already very small, will also decrease. Put another way, total spending on such categories as O&M, where DoD spends relatively large proportions of its dollars with small businesses, has diminished, whereas that for weapon-system procurement, where it spends few dollars with small businesses, is projected to increase slightly after FY 2014 (albeit after several years of decreases). As a result, the mix of DoD expenditures may become more unfavorable for small businesses.

Complicating this challenge to small-business goals is the adoption of proven business practices to reduce total costs, such as strategic sourcing, which may lead to consolidation of supply and hence increased contracting with larger businesses. For example, enterprises, in rationalizing their requirements and contracts, may consolidate their requirements in a way that leverages their purchase dollars but also in a way that exceeds the capability of a small business (or one that would remain small). Similarly, enterprises, in developing longer-term relationships and contracts with key suppliers and in providing incentives or help for suppliers to continually improve, may do so in a way that, at the least, leads to small businesses growing beyond specified size thresholds.

There are ways to implement strategic-sourcing practices that support contracting with small businesses. These may include consolidating contracts with small businesses, particularly across purchase offices or categories of goods and services. In this document, we examine both the challenges of meeting future small-business goals and how strategic-sourcing practices might help DoD meet them. Strategic sourcing can help if carefully done and, particularly, if DoD analyzes small-business spending, use, availability, capabilities, and thresholds when implementing it and identifies industries and firms where increased small-business use is most feasible.

To support such efforts, we undertake several tasks in this document. In the next chapter, we provide more background on DoD small-business contracting goals, including their origins and the aims of policymakers who have implemented them over time. In the third chapter, we examine recent and prospective trends in contracting with small businesses, including more discussion of how the changing mix of DoD expenditures may pose increasing challenges to small-business procurement goals as well as how the classification of a "small" business may affect these goals. In the fourth chapter, we explore in more depth emerging best practices that leading enterprises have used to purchase goods and services, DoD adoption of these, and the challenges they may pose to small-business procurement goals, by exploring DoD purchases with specific contractors, through particular purchase offices, and in particular industries. In the fifth and concluding chapter, we suggest some prospective next steps for DoD when working to ensure that its small-business goals and strategic-sourcing goals support each other, in part by encouraging the appropriate setting of small-business size thresholds and industry definitions. An appendix provides some additional technical detail on the data we use in this analysis.

CHAPTER TWO

Origins and Intents of Small-Business Contracting Policy

Historical Background

For much of the last century, the federal government has sought to "aid, counsel, assist and protect, insofar as possible, the interests of small business concerns" (SBA, undated-b). Such policies have deep historical roots in a public ethos holding small business to be the "backbone of democracy" and free enterprise (Bean, 1996). The means to promote small business have evolved over time, from Depression-era loans to initiatives seeking to boost federal contracting with small businesses generally to those seeking to increase federal purchases from "disadvantaged" and other specific categories of small businesses.

The origin, preservation, and expansion of small-business policies lie in both Republican and Democratic administrations and Congresses. Among the first policy efforts to boost small business was antitrust legislation, which proponents contended could allow small businesses to compete equally with big businesses.

More direct efforts to assist small business arose during the Depression, particularly through the Reconstruction Finance Corporation (RFC), a creation of the Hoover administration later "adopted" by the Roosevelt administration (SBA, undated-b). The RFC, which began making direct loans to businesses in 1934, established a small small-business division

> To examine and make recommendations on applications for loans in the amount of $100,000 or less which had been . . . forwarded to Washington for final determination. The $100,000 figure was used to distinguish small business from larger enterprises ("Aid for Small Business—The Story of Federal Action," 1956).

These policies continued and had their first major effects on defense policy during World War II through efforts to help small businesses participate in war production. One such effort was the creation in 1942 of the Smaller War Plants Corporation (SWPC) to provide direct loans to private entrepreneurs, encourage financial institutions to provide credit to small businesses, and advocate contracting with small businesses by federal procurement agencies and big businesses (Bean, 1996).

The SWPC appears to have been the first federal policy to use number of employees to define "small" businesses, deeming such businesses to be those with no more than 500 employees. Exactly how Congress selected this threshold is unclear; two historians of small-business policy have called it "arbitrary" (Bean, 2001; Berthoff, 1980/2003). Federal regulations also gave World War II contracting offices the discretion "to consider the relative size of a firm within the industry and treat it as large or small accordingly" (*Federal Register*, 1944, p. 6669).

The Reconversion Act of 1944 reduced the SWPC size threshold, defining a small plant as "any small business concern engaged primarily in production or manufacturing either employing 250 wage earners or less or coming within such other categories as may be established in consultation with the [SWPC]" (U.S. House of Representatives Select Committee on Small Business, 1952). The additional categories the SWPC could consider in defining a small business included "comparative sizes of establishments in a particular industry . . . sales volumes, quantities of materials consumed, capital investments [and] other [characteristics] reasonably attributable to small plants" (U.S. House of Representatives Select Committee on Small Business, 1952).

In 1948, Congress defined a "small" business as one without a "dominant" position in its trade or industry, having no more than 500 employees, and "independently owned and operated" (U.S. House of Representatives Select Committee on Small Business, 1952). For data-gathering purposes, however, other thresholds were common (Dilger, 2012). The Bureau of Labor Statistics, for example, considered all firms below the average sales or employment volume in an industry to be small. The U.S. Census Bureau at the time classified manufacturing firms as small if they had fewer than 100 employees, wholesalers as small if they had annual sales below $200,000, and retailers as small if they had annual sales below $50,000.

DoD and the General Services Administration used the 500-employee threshold for determining what constituted a small business but made no attempt to determine whether a particular concern was dominant in its field. DoD procurement regulations in the late 1940s also included a policy that each branch "place with small business concerns ([defined] to be any concern which employs fewer than 500 persons) a fair proportion of the total procurement of supplies and services" (*Federal Register*, 1948).

Exactly what constituted a "fair proportion" of procurement appears to have remained undefined until 1952, when Congress suggested that a "specific small-business procurement target of at least 35 percent or more of the dollar volume of military purchases is reasonable and attainable" (U.S. House of Representatives Select Committee on Small Business, 1952). Such a target not only exceeds what DoD has since spent with small businesses, it likely exceeded what the SWPC itself was able to give to small businesses during World War II (Moore et al., 2008; Berthoff, 1980/2003).

Still more important, this initial procurement goal of 35 percent was suggested in an era when Congress was recommending that extraordinary discretion be used in defining small business. The Small Defense Plants Administration (SDPA), established during the Korean War to carry out much of the same work as the earlier SWPC, had flexible standards, ranging up to 2,500 employees for firms that were independent but did not dominate their industry (Bean, 2001). Similarly, the National Production Authority's Office of Small Business proposed a three-tier size standard for manufacturing (Dilger, 2012). Under this standard, firms with fewer than 50 employees were small, those with more than 2,500 employees were large, and those with 50 to 2,500 employees were classified as small or large depending on the structure of their industry.

In the early 1950s, Congress, in seeking to design more general small-business legislation, explicitly rejected

> any attempt to formulate a rigid definition of small business. It believe[d] that the concept of small business must remain flexible and adaptable to the peculiar needs of each instance in which a definition may be required . . . the essential thing is to understand the *problem*

[emphasis in original] of small business. This is to maintain the vigor of the competitive system, to assure free opportunity to establish a new business and to grow [and] to give the smaller concerns an even break. For legal and administrative purposes, a rather precise definition may at times be necessary. But it is clear that such a definition must be somewhat arbitrary as objective criteria . . . simply do not exist . . . whatever limits may be established to the category of small business, they must vary from industry according to the general industrial pattern of each. Public policy may demand similar treatment for a firm of 2,500 employees in one industry as it does for a firm of only 50 employees in another (U.S. House of Representatives Select Committee on Small Business, 1952).

Yet the military refused to recognize the SDPA and other flexible classifications, continuing to define a small business as one with fewer than 500 employees. This, one historian (Bean, 2001) suggests, was meant to limit the interference of the SDPA in the procurement process.

Efforts to boost small-business contracts for defense procurement were also complicated by the concentration of large corporations in heavy industry and by the ability of small business to realize greater rewards from its flexibility in the civilian sector (Bean, 1996). They may also have been complicated by the diffuse interests of small businesses, with many small-business owners having more common interests with others in their industry than with other small businesses generally. Still, the "symbolism" of small business made it difficult for legislators to vote against small-business legislation (Bean, 1996, p. 168).

Hence, small-business legislation usually passed with near-unanimous votes. The Eisenhower administration, when abolishing the RFC, retained its small-business purposes through creation of SBA. In addition to supporting the interests of small-business concerns, the SBA charter also reiterated previous congressional calls that a "fair proportion" of government contracts and sales of surplus property go to small businesses.

Varying Definitions of Small Business: Differences by Policy

The Small Business Act of 1953 specified two criteria by which a business might be considered small: independently owned and operated and not dominant in its field (Public Law 85-536, 2013). Beyond that, it largely left to the discretion of the SBA administrator the criteria by which a concern might be considered small. The act noted that number of employees, dollar volume of business, and net income could be among the standards used to determine whether a business was small.

Initially, SBA had two sets of size standards: one for procurement preferences and the other for financial and other assistance (*Federal Register*, 1956). The procurement standard specified a small business as a concern "that (1) is not dominant in its field of operation and, with its affiliates, employs fewer than 500 employees, or (2) is certified as a small business concern by SBA" (*Federal Register*, 1956, p. 9710). Firms with more than 500 employees could also qualify as small businesses as long as SBA determined that "the applicant, together with all its affiliates, is not dominant and is otherwise determined to be a small business in its field of operation" (*Federal Register*, 1956, p. 9710). Firms that were determined to be "dominant" could not be certified as small businesses, even if they had fewer than 500 employees. The emphasis on 500 employees drew some opposition, including testimony that congressional intent was to have a standard that varied by industry, as well as objections to having different standards for manufacturing and other purposes (Dilger, 2012).

The standard for financial or other assistance has differed by industry. Manufacturers were small if they had no more than 250 employees, large if they had more than 1,000 employees, and small or large, depending on the industry, if employing more than 250 employees but no more than 1,000 employees. Other thresholds included $5,000,000 in annual sales for wholesalers, $1,000,000 in annual receipts for service trades, and $5,000,000 in annual receipts (as averaged over three years) for construction trades. The use of number of employees for manufacturers and sales or receipts for other industries would eventually be adopted for procurement as well. The reason for this, as congressional testimony of the time noted, was a belief that the size of nonmanufacturing firms had more to do with sales or receipts than employees (Dilger, 2012).

More generally, over time, employee-size thresholds have been typically used in manufacturing and other industries that have high capital requirements, low operational costs relative to receipts, variation of firms by stage of production or degree of vertical integration, or horizontally structured firms (SBA, 2009). Receipt-size thresholds are typical in industries that have high levels of labor requirements, subcontracting, and part-time or seasonal employment. A few industries over time have developed mixed employee and receipt thresholds.

Other legislation has used different, typically smaller, thresholds. Congress has used many criteria to define small businesses that it wished to exempt from legislative requirements (Keefe, Gates, and Talley, 2007). Table 2.1 lists these for several significant regulations. Some acts, such as the Small Business Regulatory Enforcement Fairness Act of 1996, use the same thresholds of the Small Business Act. Some, such as the Paperwork Reduction Act, use both the thresholds of the Small Business Act as well as an exception, such as 25 employees for all firms regardless of their classification under other (e.g., receipt) threshold standards.

Table 2.1
Size of Small-Business Exemptions for Major Legislative Acts

Act	Year	Threshold for Defining Small Business
Securities Exchange Act	1934	500 stockholders and less than $1 million in assets
Fair Labor Standards	1938	$500,000 in gross sales
Civil Rights	1964	Firms with 15 or fewer employees are exempt from record keeping
Age Discrimination in Employment	1967	20 employees
Occupational Safety and Health	1970	10 employees
Subchapter S Revision	1982	75 shareholders
Consolidated Omnibus Budget Reconciliation	1986	20 employees
Worker Adjustment and Retraining Notification	1988	100 employees
Americans with Disabilities	1990	15 employees
Family and Medical Leave	1993	50 employees within a 75-mile radius
Food and Drug Administration Modernization	1997	$500,000 in sales or no more than $50,000 in sales of food to consumers

SOURCE: Keefe, Gates, and Talley (2007).

Changes in Small-Business Activity over Time

The meaning and relevance of thresholds can change over time. The most common threshold used for procurement preference over time has remained that of 500 employees. Yet the relevance of that threshold for defining relatively small businesses has changed in recent decades.

For example, from the late 1950s to the late 1990s, the share of economic activity for firms with fewer than 500 employees decreased markedly. Specifically, such small firms accounted for 57 percent of the private nonfarm gross domestic product in 1958 but for only 50 percent in 1997 (Joel Popkin and Company, 2001). During this time, small businesses remained most prevalent in construction but declined in mining and manufacturing as well as in services (Figure 2.1).

There is some evidence that the small-business share of U.S. economic activity has continued to decrease. Specifically, from 1998 to 2010, the small-business share of gross domestic product decreased from 51 percent to 45 percent (Kobe, 2012).[1] The decrease was particularly sharp in professional and technical services (Figure 2.2). Economic Census data on industry receipts by number of employees in a firm show similar patterns.[2] Firms with fewer than 500 employees accounted for 41 percent of all receipts for all firms across all industries in 1997 but for 38 percent in 2007 (U.S. Census Bureau, annual).

Such trends may be attributable in part to general industry consolidation that often occurs over time. Deans, Kroeger, and Zeisel (2002) suggest a four-stage ongoing and accelerating process of industry consolidation. The four stages for this are opening, scale, focus, and balance and alliance (Figure 2.3). Industries become more diffuse in initial stages but highly concentrated in later stages. Among the most concentrated industries they identified at the time are Defense, Shipbuilding, Aircraft Original Equipment Manufacturers and Aerospace Suppliers.[3]

---

[1]   Unfortunately, data on small-business shares of gross domestic product are not strictly comparable over time for several reasons. We note three of these below.

First, the change from the Standard Industrial Classification (SIC) to the NAICS for analyzing economic activity by industry limits attempts to compare activity by sector and size of firm. Generally speaking, SIC data are available through the late 1990s, and NAICS data since then, but comparisons of data gathered under the two systems are difficult or, in many circumstances, impossible. For more discussion on this problem and some baseline analyses comparing small-business activity by sectors defined by these two classification systems, see Joel Popkin and Company (2002).

Second, methods for calculating the small-business share of economic activity have changed in how they consider sole proprietorships or partnerships. For years before 2002, such calculations assumed that all sole proprietorships and partnerships were small businesses. Subsequent efforts to estimate the small-business share of the economy has sought to adjust for partnerships and, particularly, for limited-liability companies (LLCs) that are not small businesses. For more discussion of such adjustments and of how including LLCs would inflate recent levels of economic activity attributable to small business, see Kobe (2012), especially pp. 15–18.

Third, at the time of the most recent effort to estimate the small-business share of gross domestic product, the source data were complete through 2008. As a result, estimates for subsequent years are preliminary. For more discussion of this issue, see Kobe (2012), especially pp. 21–24.

[2]   Conducted in years ending in 2 and 7, the Economic Census gathers data by establishment and aggregates, by firm, numbers of employees, and annual receipts. Data are classified by NAICS codes. For more on the Economic Census and its methods, see U.S. Census Bureau (2009a).

[3]   For further discussion on industry consolidation over time, see A. T. Kearney, Inc. (2001). For discussion on consolidation in defense industries, see General Accounting Office (1988) and Gansler (2011). For discussion on industry consolidation trends and federal contract bundling, see Baldwin, Camm, and Moore (2001).

Figure 2.1
Share of Private Nonfarm Gross Domestic Product for Firms with Fewer than 500 Employees, 1958 and 1997

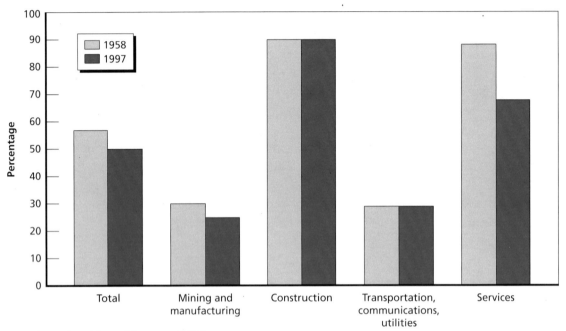

SOURCE: Joel Popkin and Company (2001).
RAND RR410-2.1

Figure 2.2
Share of Economic Activity for Firms with Fewer than 500 Employees, 1998 and 2010

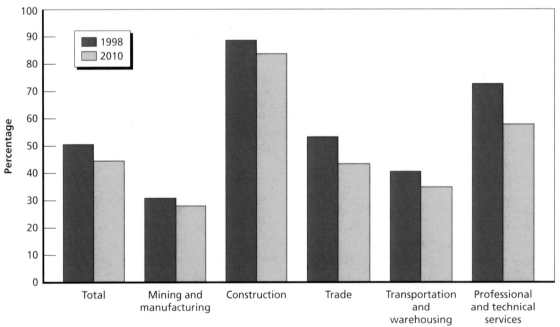

SOURCE: Kobe (2012).
RAND RR410-2.2

Figure 2.3
Industry Growth and Consolidation Curve

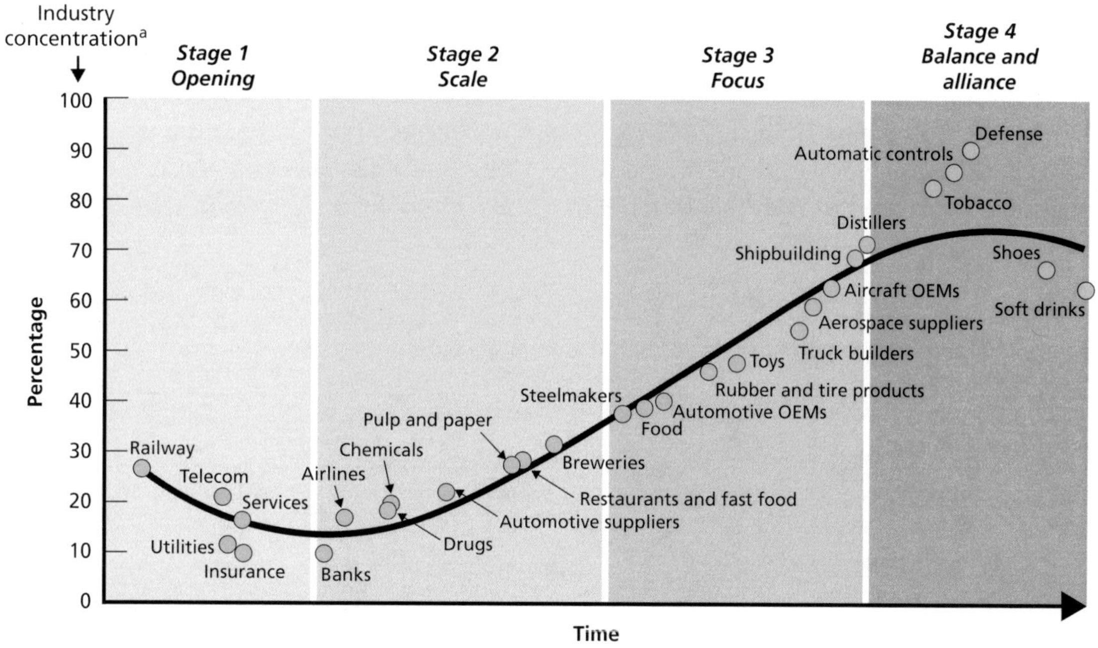

SOURCE: Deans, Kroeger, and Zeisel (2002).
[a]This is the combined market share of the three largest companies in an industry.

Past Proposals to Change Size Thresholds

SBA continues to use the benchmark of 500 employees as one of its anchor size standards when setting size thresholds.[4] This number is still used in most industries in which number of employees is used to determine size, particularly in manufacturing (13 CFR §121, annual).[5] SBA continues to consider the 500-employee threshold sufficient for "fostering competition within the economy by enabling businesses beyond the start-up phase" and for focusing small-business aid on firms that were "still small relative to the leading producers in the industry" (SBA, 2009).

SBA considers a variety of characteristics in determining whether to use number of employees or firm receipts as an industry size threshold (SBA, 2009). Characteristics that favor using number of employees include high capital requirements, low operational costs relative to receipts, variance of firms in supply chain, and horizontally structured firms. Those that favor using firm receipts include labor intensiveness, ease of factor substitution, presence of

---

[4]   The anchor size standards are not minimum size standards but are rather, as noted, benchmarks or starting points from which SBA considers exceptions to the anchor standard. To the extent that characteristics of one industry differ from others with the same anchor size standard, SBA may choose to set a size standard higher, or lower. For further discussion, see SBA (2009).

[5]   The Code of Federal Regulations (CFR) lists small-business size thresholds by six-digit NAICS codes. (When industries were classified by the SIC, the CFR listed small-business size thresholds by four-digit SIC codes.) Although the small-business size threshold for most industries reflects an anchor threshold, any exceptions to these would typically be determined on the basis of the six-digit NAICS code.

subcontracting,[6] part-time or seasonal employees, and operations in multiple locations. Table 2.2 summarizes these.

SBA will recognize changing conditions, both across the economy and within specific industries, to change size thresholds. Proposals to change size standards, however, can draw strong opposition.[7]

A 1980 proposal sought to have an employee-size standard for nearly all industries and small-business programs (Dilger, 2012). Among the reasons SBA cited for the proposal was comparability across industries and the undermining of receipts-based standards by inflation and a subsequent need to revise such standards. The 1980 proposal would have set employee-

Table 2.2
Industry Characteristic Supporting Use of Employee- or Receipts-based Size Measures

Industry Characteristic	Employees or Receipts	Comment
High capital requirements	Employees	Assumes that the level of employment varies with that of production and that the value of output is largely derived from fixed assets
Low operational costs relative to receipts	Employees	Assumes that low labor inputs generate large receipts
Variance of firms in supply chain	Employees	Especially in industries where the number of employees is more strongly correlated to value added than to receipts
Horizontally structured firms	Employees	Varying receipts-to-employees relationships among firms
Labor-intensive	Receipts	Output value varies with employment level
Ease of factor substitution	Receipts	Same output can be produced by varying labor and capital
Presence of subcontracting	Receipts	Same output can be produced with differing levels of outsourcing
Part-time or seasonal employees	Receipts	Same output can be produced with differing employment practices
Operating in multiple industries	Receipts	Receipts are assumed to provide a more homogeneous measure of size than number of employees

SOURCE: SBA (2009).

---

[6] In interviews with representatives of small and other-than-small businesses regarding ways to determine business size for policy purposes, we heard several claim that subcontracts often represent "pass-through" costs that raise the price of a contract and therefore firm receipts but do not increase firm profits or number of employees. For example a representative of a small Engineering Services firm whom we interviewed noted that about half of the firm's revenues for government work are pass-through costs boosting receipts but not profits. On one project, this representative claimed, the firm spent about a half-million dollars on labor but millions more on materials. Materials costs are often considered in setting size thresholds in manufacturing and industries with employee-based thresholds but not typically for services industries such as engineering services.

[7] SBA also notes that size standards "must be above the entry-level because Federal government contracting requirements usually cannot be met by a new or very small firm" (SBA, 2009). Yet, there are limits to how SBA will use firm size in setting thresholds levels. It will not, for example, "designate a size standard for the Federal contracting factor that is higher than two levels above the current size standard because this would result, in most cases, in designating a size standard more than twice the current size standard" (SBA, 2009). We infer from this that SBA does not seek radical change to size standards.

size standards from 15 to 2,500 employees depending on whether an industry was concentrated, competitive, or mixed, with higher size standards for more concentrated industries.

Of the more than 1,500 public comments SBA received on this proposal, more than 86 percent criticized it, with most criticism coming from firms that would no longer be considered small (Dilger, 2012). Several federal agencies, including DoD, also said that the proposed thresholds were too low for procurement purposes. SBA gained greater support for subsequent proposals that restored small-business eligibility to some industries that would have been excluded by the original proposal, that narrowed the range of thresholds from 25 to 500 employees, and that used the same thresholds for both procurement preferences and other small-business programs.

A 1985 congressional proposal sought to adjust small-business size standards based on the share that small businesses had in an industry as well as the share such businesses had of federal procurement (Dilger, 2012). Specifically, the legislation would have required a 20 percent reduction in the threshold if small businesses had at least 60 percent of the market in an industry and at least 40 percent of their market share was achieved through federal procurement contracts. Conversely, the legislation would have increased thresholds for industries in which small businesses had less than 20 percent of the market in an industry, and less than 10 percent of their market share was achieved through federal procurement contracts. SBA, trade associations, and federal procurement officials opposed this legislation, which was not reported out of committee.

SBA again proposed to streamline thresholds in 1992 (Dilger, 2012). The proposal would have replaced the 30 different size standards then extant with nine, five of which were employee-based (ranging from 100 to 1,500 employees) and four of which were revenue-based (ranging from $5 million to $24 million in annual receipts). The proposal was ultimately withdrawn, given perceived anomalies in the receipts standards but, over time, SBA would adjust its receipts-standards for inflation.

In 2004, SBA once again proposed to use employee-size thresholds for all industries (Dilger, 2012). By this time 37 different size standards were being used across nearly 1,200 industries and subindustry activities. The proposal would not have changed any employee-size standards then used but would have converted size standards based on other measures to employee-size standards. Although most comments supported the rule, a large number objected to parts of it, and congressional leaders objected to actions that would reduce the number of businesses considered to be small.

Receipts-based thresholds have faced different issues over time. In 1954, SBA established a threshold of $1 million in average annual receipts for loan programs in nonmanufacturing industries. This became the anchor standard with receipts-based size standards, with higher thresholds set in some industries, such as construction. SBA has expressed a general preference for "receipts as a size measure because it measures the value of output of a business and can be easily verified by business tax returns and financial records" (SBA, 2009).

Over time, the $1 million anchor standard has evolved to $7 million. This standard has not always kept pace with inflation (Figure 2.4), much less with industry consolidation. For example, a $1 million threshold in 1963, the first year in which we found this threshold specified for procurement programs as well, if adjusted annually for inflation would have been about $9 million in recent years.

SBA also makes adjustments and exceptions within industries. For example, its current receipts-based threshold for Engineering Services (NAICS code 541330) is twofold, with a

Figure 2.4
Traditional Anchor Size Standard for Receipts-Based Industries, 1963 to 2012

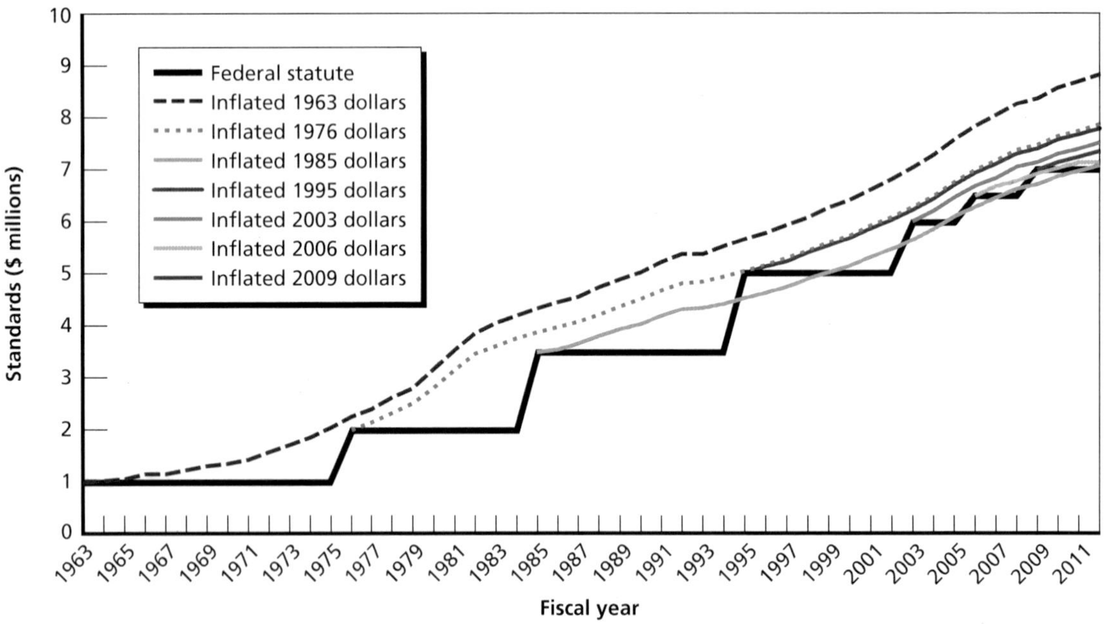

SOURCES: Thresholds are as reported in 13 CFR §121 (annual). Inflated dollars are calculated using 2012 deflators in U.S. Department of Defense (2012).
RAND RR410-2.4

base threshold of $14.0 million in annual receipts but $35.5 million for Marine Engineering and Naval Architecture services, engineering services for Military and Aerospace Equipment and Military Weapons, and contracts for Engineering Services Awarded Under the National Energy Policy Act of 1992.

The exception for Marine Engineering and Naval Architecture services is one of the oldest the government has for procurement purposes. It first appears in the CFR in 1996 at $5 million, when the anchor standard was still $1 million in annual receipts. Here, too, inflation has eroded the real value of the thresholds over time, although recent adjustments have recaptured some of this lost value (Figure 2.5). The original $5 million exception instituted in 1966, if annually adjusted for inflation, would now be about $39 million, whereas the 1967 adjustment, if subsequently adjusted for inflation, would now be more than $45 million in annual receipts.

Perhaps further eroding the value of such thresholds for the military is the increasing complexity, and expense, of military ships. Arena et al. (2006) note that annual cost escalation for amphibious ships, surface combatants, attack submarines, and nuclear aircraft carriers has ranged from 7 to 11 percent in recent decades, compared to 4 to 5 percent for general inflation indices. They attribute this difference in large part to the Navy's desire for larger and more complex ships.

Different Data Perspectives on Industries and Small Businesses

A further, albeit more technical, problem with small-business thresholds lies in the data used to establish them. In considering whether to adjust the threshold from the anchor for a given

Figure 2.5
Small-Business Size Threshold for Procurement of Marine Engineering and Naval Architecture Services, 1966 to 2012

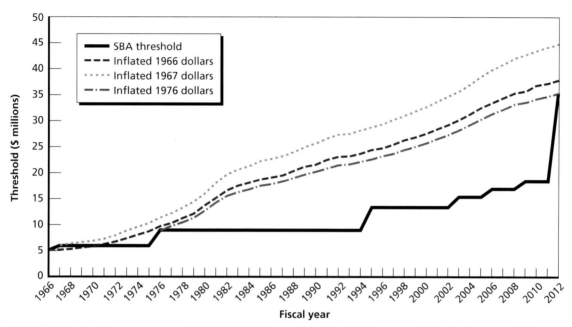

SOURCES: Thresholds are as reported in 13 CFR §121 (annual). Inflated dollars are calculated using 2012 deflators in U.S. Department of Defense (2012).
RAND *RR410-2.5*

industry, SBA analyzes, among other things, special tabulations of firm-level data from the Economic Census conducted every five years. Among other variables, the Economic Census provides industry data by six-digit NAICS codes on the distribution of firms by receipt- and employment-size categories, as well as by annual total receipts. Ideally, these data can be used to show total economic activity within an industry as well as that of small businesses within it.

Yet it is not clear whether the data SBA uses always provide a complete and accurate picture, especially in industries of great concern to DoD. Table 2.3 presents characteristics in 2002 and 2007 of two industries important to DoD: Ammunition (Except Small Arms) Manufacturing (NAICS code 332993) and Military Armored Vehicle, Tank, and Tank Component Manufacturing (NAICS code 336992). These industries are noteworthy not only for the inherent military character of their goods and services but also for the far greater size found for these industries evident in the Federal Procurement Data System (FPDS) than is evident in the Economic Census. (For more on our calculations regarding these industries, see the appendix.)

The special Economic Census indicates that total annual receipts in Ammunition (Except Small Arms) Manufacturing (332951) in 2002 totaled $1.19 billion, and contract-action data from the FPDS indicate that DoD spent $1.89 billion in FY 2002 in this industry.[8] In 2007, total sales in this industry, as reported in the Economic Census, had increased to $1.75 billion,

---

[8]   More specifically, contract-action data indicate that DoD spent $1.89 billion in goaling dollars in this industry. As we discuss in the next chapter, such dollars understate both total DoD expenditures in an industry as well as DoD expenditures within the United States. Within the United States, for example, "goaling" dollars exclude purchases of goods and services from educational or nonprofit organizations,

Table 2.3
Characteristics of Ammunition and Military Armored Vehicle Manufacturing Industries in Calendar/ Fiscal Years 2002 and 2007

	Ammunition (Except Small Arms) Manufacturing (NAICS Code 332993)	Military Armored Vehicle, Tank, and Tank Component Manufacturing (NAICS Code 336992)
Reported industry receipts ($ billions), per Economic Census		
2002	$1.19	$1.51
2007	$1.75	$5.52
DoD goaling-dollar procurement in industry ($ billions), per FPDS		
2002	$1.89	$1.94
2007	$2.15	$11.57
Percentage of industry revenues to small business, per Economic Census		
2002	28.1%	10.5%
2007	32.4%	8.7%
Percentage of DoD procurement with small business, per FPDS goaling-dollar data		
2002	12.2%	3.1%
2007	22.3%	3.9%

SOURCE: RAND calculations using FPDS and Economic Census data.

but DoD procurement increased still more, to $2.15 billion. Similarly, although the Economic Census in 2002 indicated that there were $1.51 billion in receipts for Military Armored Vehicle Manufacturing (336992), contract-action data indicate that DoD spent $1.94 billion in it that year. Likewise, whereas this industry had grown to $5.52 billion in receipts by 2007, contract-action data indicated that DoD spent at least $11.57 billion. Put another way, the Economic Census statistics account for only about half to three-fourths of DoD purchases alone in the industry. The Economic Census data apparently do not account for all DoD purchases, much less for whatever nonmilitary purchases there may be in these industries. They also did not fully account for growth in Military Armored Vehicle Manufacturing, which, as with that in Ammunition (Except Small Arms) Manufacturing, we surmise occurred because of military actions in Iraq and Afghanistan.

Similar differences exist in the reported levels of small-business participation in each industry. Given what we surmise is DoD's dominant position in these industries, these differences are particularly troubling for efforts to set small-business size thresholds in them. In 2002, the Economic Census found that 28.1 percent of receipts in the Ammunition Manufacturing industry went to small businesses but contract-action data show that only 12.2 percent went to such businesses. By 2007, DoD procurement in this industry increased to 22.3 percent, but the Economic Census showed that small businesses comprised 32.4 percent of industry receipts. Similarly, in 2002, the Economic Census found that 10.5 percent of receipts for the

Military Armored Vehicle Manufacturing went to small businesses, but contract-action data indicate that DoD spent only 3.1 percent of its dollars in this industry with such businesses. By 2007, DoD purchases in this industry from small businesses had increased to 3.9 percent, but Economic Census data were still showing that such businesses accounted for 8.7 percent of receipts in the industry. Regardless, our point is not so much to determine the actual presence of small business in these industries and how this has changed over time but to illustrate how two sources of data diverge so much on the shape of these industries.

As noted, we strongly suspect that, in these two industries, the Economic Census may be understating their actual size and overstating the prevalence of small businesses within them. This, in turn, may inadvertently lead to erroneous conclusions about what are small businesses in these industries and the proper thresholds for defining them.

Classifying Industries Correctly

An additional problem with Economic Census data is that their classifications, even if accurate at the level of a six-digit NAICS code, can be very broad. For example, Aircraft Manufacturing (NAICS code 336411) includes not only aircraft manufacturing but also aircraft conversions (e.g., major system modifications), aircraft overhauling, aircraft rebuilding, autogiro manufacturing, blimp manufacturing, developing and producing prototypes for aircraft, glider manufacturing, hang-glider manufacturing, helicopter manufacturing, drone manufacturing, and ultra-light aircraft manufacturing—all representing products of widely varying value to and uses by DoD. Such goods and services may also typically be produced by firms of greatly different sizes. Contract-action data indicate that most DoD purchases in this industry are for aircraft or airframe structural components and that most categories of goods and services encompassed in this industry account for a very small proportion of DoD expenditures.

Put another way, Economic Census data on the Aircraft Manufacturing industry may overstate what is truly relevant for DoD purposes. To the extent that this industry includes goods and services not relevant to DoD needs, and especially to the extent that such less relevant goods and services will be produced by smaller firms, Economic Census data will show an industry that has skewed distributions for defining small businesses. Such data effectively equate, for example, manufacturers of hang gliders with those of fighter aircraft for determining what is a small business within the industry. It is also not clear whether threshold adjustments always reflect changes to defense-dominated industries and how these may be reshaped by evolving needs. For example, it is increasingly common for firms to buy goods and services together (Moore, Grammich, and Bickel, 2007). This can reshape the character of sales within an industry as well as the effective size of a business needed to compete successfully—and therefore what constitutes a "small" business within an industry.

Still other external events can reshape an industry and what might be a small business within it. For example, the threshold for Ammunition (Except Small Arms) Manufacturing (NAICS code 332993) has remained at 1,500 employees since 1972. In the four decades since, the U.S. military has withdrawn from Vietnam, conducted a defense buildup peaking in 1985 to counter the Soviet threat, fought two wars in Iraq, and conducted antiterror operations around the world. With changes in military operations and weaponry, we surmise that the composition of this industry has changed over time. Statistics of U.S. Businesses (U.S. Census Bureau, 2013) indicate that the number of firms in this industry has decreased from 59 with

79 establishments in 1992, shortly after the end of the Cold War, to 39 firms with 46 establishments in 2012 (U.S. Census Bureau, annual).[9]

Firms may have activities in multiple industries but be recorded only in one industry in Economic Census data. Firms engaged in distinctly different lines of activity (e.g., working in more than one industry) at one location are requested to submit separate reports to the Economic Census—if their records permit such a separation, which is not always the case. Unless firms keep their business records by Census Bureau industrial classifications, rather than those they find best for their own management, this request is likely to go unfulfilled (as we learned in correspondence with Census Bureau researchers). Consider, for example, a firm with three establishments, the first of which works in three industries, the second that works in two more, and the third establishment that works in yet another industry accounting for most firm revenues. The industry of the third establishment will be considered the industry for the firm as a whole in Economic Census data, but the firm may legitimately claim to work in other industries as well.

In contrast to the Economic Census, the FPDS records the six-digit NAICS code reflecting the industry in which goods or services are purchased. Depending on the circumstances of how the FPDS data are completed, it is conceivable that the industry recorded in the FPDS need not reflect the predominant industry a firm reports to the Economic Census. Indeed, the System for Award Management, in which all federal contractors must register, allows firms to register in hundreds of different industries (each with its own small-business size threshold). Presumably, a DoD procurement officer records the industry that appears most logical for the transaction, and an establishment or firm representative records its predominant industry for all its revenue when completing an Economic Census form, even though the firm might provide goods and services in a number of industries.

Because a number of firms report only their predominant industry every five years to the Economic Census, whereas the FPDS reports the industry for the specific purchase at the time of contract award, specific industry revenues may not match. This can be particularly noticeable in industries where DoD purchasing predominates and the industry is not the predominant industry of some of the firms providing the specific good or service.

Implications: Small Business Is a Qualitative Concept Difficult to Define Quantitatively

Small business is a qualitative concept that, for policy purposes, is defined quantitatively. In devising small-business legislation, Congress has declined to define a small business, recognizing that the size of what should be considered a small business may vary based on the purpose of a given program, whether it be loans, implementation of regulations, or other policy mandates. Historically, the most common threshold for defining small businesses in procurement-

---

[9]   The U.S. Census Bureau defines an establishment as "[a] single physical location where business is conducted, or where services are performed" and a firm as "[a] business organization or entity consisting of one or more domestic establishment locations under common ownership or control" (U.S. Census Bureau, 2009b). Put another way, a firm may comprise multiple establishments. For example, a chain store under single ownership with five locations would be one firm with five establishments. Although the Economic Census collects data by both firm and establishment, it is firm-level data that determine whether an industry is a small business as well as the industry in which it might be a small business.

preference programs has been 500 employees. Yet why this standard was chosen, or why it persists, is not clear.

Over time, policymakers have chosen different thresholds for different purposes. SBA has also occasionally revised thresholds, particularly for receipts-based industries. SBA adjustments, although more frequent in recent years, have not historically kept pace with inflation. They also might not account for increasing complexity or consolidation in some industries.

The data SBA uses to assess the prevalence of small businesses within industries may not be as comprehensive or accurate as they should be, a topic that we discuss below. For some defense-related industries, the Economic Census appears to misstate total industry size or the portion relevant to DoD and to misstate the prevalence of small businesses within them.

Although there are and have been problems with small-business definitions for policy purposes, DoD will have to continue to meet small-business goals. With knowledge of how these goals have evolved and the purposes they have sought to serve, policymakers may, in future years, seek thresholds that better reflect the broader purpose of such goals. For now, however, we turn to a more immediate need of avoiding contradiction between small-business goals and those sought through strategic sourcing.

CHAPTER THREE

Composition of Small-Business Purchases by DoD and Its Implications for Strategic Sourcing

Small-Business Dollars and Contracts

As noted above, Congress has established a goal that 23 percent of all federal dollars on prime contracts be spent with small businesses. To achieve this goal, every two years SBA works with each federal agency to set an agency-specific goal (SBA, undated-c). SBA ensures that the sum total of these goals, if met, would exceed the 23 percent government-wide target. The most recent goal that SBA negotiated with DoD calls for 22.50 percent of DoD prime-contract dollars to be spent with small businesses (Office of Small Business Programs, undated-b).

In recent years, DoD has spent more than $350 billion annually on prime-contract purchases. However, not all these purchases are subject to small-business procurement goals. Rather, only a subset of them, referred to as "goaling" dollars, is subject to the goal. Small-business goaling dollars are those that federal authorities consider when determining goals for each agency. Goaling dollars exclude, among other categories, foreign military sales and purchases from foreign concerns, educational or nonprofit organizations, and Federal Prison Industries, Inc. (also known as UNICOR). Overall, as Figure 3.1 indicates, about 80 percent of DoD prime-contract dollars are considered for small-business goals, and more than 90 percent of small-business purchases are spent on goaling-dollar categories. (For more on our methods in analyzing FPDS data, see the appendix.)

In FY 2012, DoD spent 20 percent of its prime-contract dollars with small businesses, and such businesses accounted for 71 percent of contracts written or used that year. Using such a large number of contracts for a relatively small portion of expenditures increases workload and hence requirements for contracting personnel. Below, we explore the implications of high numbers of contracts for strategic-sourcing initiatives.

Changing Composition of Small-Business Purchases

One challenge that DoD will face in meeting small-business goals, as noted above, is the changing composition of its purchases. To illustrate this, we present DoD expenditures in five categories and the percentage of prime-contract dollars in each of them that went to small businesses in FY 2012 (Table 3.1).

Small-business procurement policy appears to implicitly assume that such businesses make goods and services in the same proportion that all businesses do and that the economy demands. Yet it is not clear that small businesses would make, for example, weapon systems

Figure 3.1
DoD Prime-Contract (Then-Year) Dollars, Total and Spent with Small Businesses, by Goaling Status, FY 2005 to FY 2012

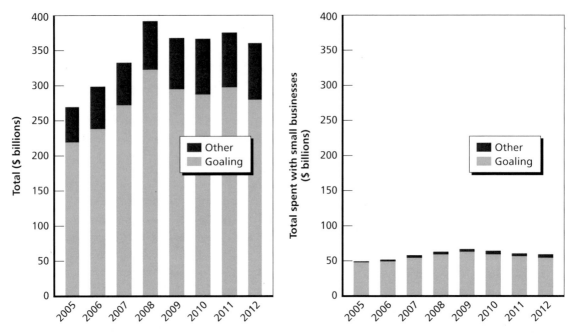

SOURCE: RAND analysis of FPDS-NG data.
RAND RR410-3.1

Table 3.1
DoD Expenditures, and Small-Business Share of Prime Contracts, by Category, FY 2012

Category	% of Goaling Dollars	% of Prime-Contract Dollars Going to Small Businesses
Operations and Maintenance	*49.1*	*27.0*
Procurement	29.2	6.2
Research, Test, Development, and Evaluation	14.9	14.1
Military Construction	3.7	40.1
Family Housing	0.1	63.8
U.S. Army Corps of Engineers, Civil Works[a]	1.8	48.5
Non-DoD[a]	0.6	17.4
Total for all categories	100	
Average across all categories		19.2

SOURCES: Office of the Under Secretary of Defense (Comptroller) (2012); RAND analysis of FPDS-NG data.

[a] Represent categories over which DoD has no control regarding the amount or distribution but which do count toward meeting DoD small-business goals. Such funds might include Homeland Security funds spent through the Army Corps of Engineers for border fencing or White House or State Department funds spent through DoD for other purposes.

in the same proportion that the overall economy does. At the same time, small businesses may be more prevalent in some fields where entry barriers are lower. In four of these budget categories—Operations and Maintenance, Military Construction, Family Housing, and Civil Works, all underlined in the above table—DoD expenditures with small businesses are substantially above the agency and government-wide goals. Military Construction and Family Housing, however, constitute relatively small categories of expenditures, and Civil Works is both small and beyond the immediate control of DoD. DoD spending on O&M also underlined in Table 3.1, is considerably larger; indeed, it is the largest budget category of expenditures for DoD. Its importance for DoD small-business spending is particularly pronounced. Our analysis of FY 2012 contract-action data shows that O&M accounts for 67.5 percent of DoD spending of goaling dollars with *small businesses*—an even greater proportion than the 49.1 percent shown above for goaling dollars spent with *all* businesses in O&M. The ability of DoD to meet its small-business goals, therefore, depends critically on both overall O&M spending in general and on small-business spending within that budget category in particular.

As noted above, however, O&M spending has decreased even more than total DoD expenditures in recent years. In fact, such spending peaked in 2011 and, in FY 2014, is budgeted (in real dollars) to be 35 percent below its peak (Figure 3.2).

The decreasing share of O&M in the DoD budget poses great challenges to meeting small-business goals, as Figure 3.3 illustrates. Should small-business spending in the O&M category remain at 27.0 percent (and the proportion of spending on small businesses in other categories also remain constant), then overall DoD spending with small businesses will decrease to 17.8 percent by FY 2018. This is shown by the blue dashed line and the blue, left-hand axis in Figure 3.3. Conversely, if DoD were to meet a departmental goal of 22.5 percent by increas-

Figure 3.2
DoD Spending, by Category, Recent and Projected, FY 2006 to FY 2018

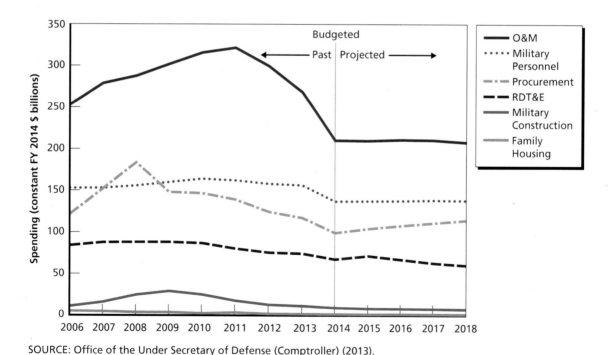

SOURCE: Office of the Under Secretary of Defense (Comptroller) (2013).
RAND *RR410-3.2*

Figure 3.3
O&M Spending and Expected Effects on Small-Business Goals, FY 2012 to FY 2018

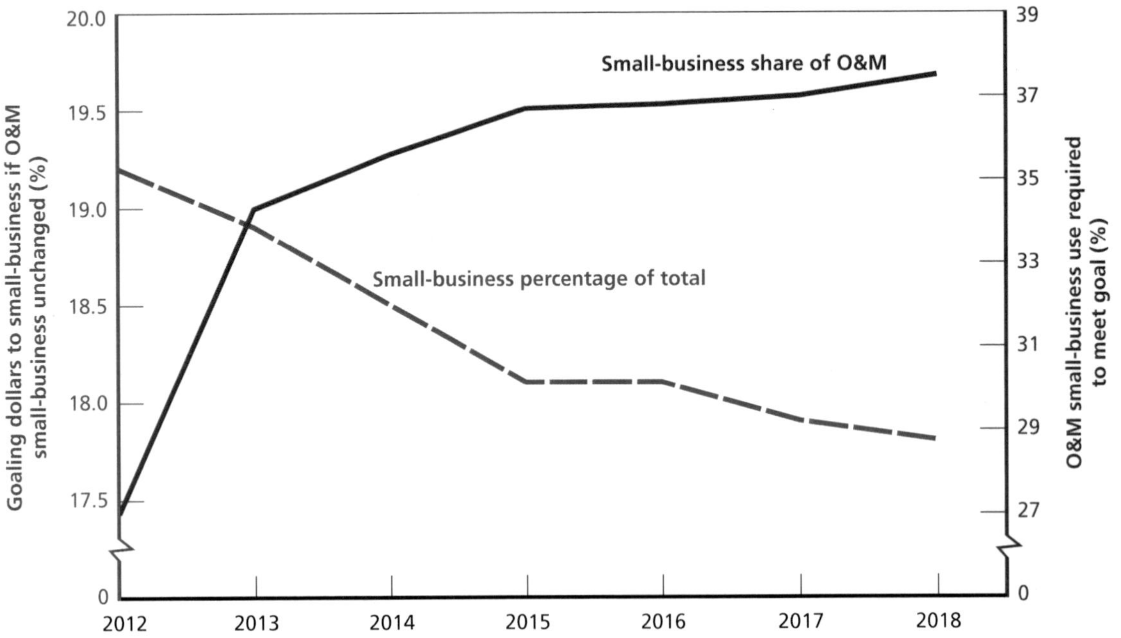

SOURCES: RAND calculations using FPDS data.
RAND *RR410-3.3*

ing small-business spending on O&M (again, assuming unchanging proportions in other categories), then it would have to increase such spending substantially, from 27.0 percent in FY 2012 to 37.5 percent in FY 2018. This is shown by the red, solid line, and the red, right-hand axis in Figure 3.3.

Small-Business Purchases, by Industry

Just as DoD small-business purchases are more concentrated in certain budget categories, so also are they more concentrated in certain industries. In fact, 45 percent of its small-business purchases (on contracts both written and used by DoD) in FY 2012 were in just ten industries, as defined by six-digit NAICS codes (Table 3.2). Of these, six—Engineering Services, Facilities Support Services, Other Computer Related Services, Petroleum Refineries, Ship Building and Repairing, and Other Aircraft Parts and Auxiliary Equipment Manufacturing—are also among the top industries from which DoD purchases O&M goods and services.

Within O&M, the budget category in which most DoD small-business purchases occur, the top ten industries accounted for $66.8 billion of goods and services in FY 2012, or 49 percent of all goaling dollars spent on O&M (Table 3.3). These have varying degrees of small-business utilization: five at 12 percent or lower and three at 39 percent or higher. The small-business thresholds within these industries also vary, from 1,000 to 1,500 employees for those with employee-based thresholds and from $7.0 million to $35.5 million for those with revenue-based thresholds. The proportion of small businesses in each industry registered in the

Table 3.2
Leading Industries for DoD Small-Business Purchases, FY 2012

NAICS Code	Industry Name	Value of DoD Small-Business Contracts[a] ($ millions)	Small-Business % of All Goaling Dollars
236220	Commercial and Institutional Building Construction	6,470	52
541712	Research and Development in the Physical, Engineering, and Life Sciences (except Biotechnology)	4,605	29
541330	Engineering Services	3,853	15
561210	Facilities Support Services	1,884	42
541519	Other Computer Related Services	1,782	39
237990	Other Heavy and Civil Engineering Construction	1,693	46
324110	Petroleum Refineries	1,354	12
562910	Remediation Services	1,121	59
336611	Ship Building and Repairing	1,004	6
336413	Other Aircraft Parts and Auxiliary Equipment Manufacturing	976	9
Total for all industries		55,189	
Average across all industries			20

SOURCE: FY 2012 FPDS data for goaling dollars.
[a] Written and used by DoD.

Central Contractor Registry (CCR) also varies widely, shaping the pool from which DoD may draw small-business suppliers.[1]

Three industries in Table 3.3 are particularly noteworthy. First, DoD uses no small businesses for Direct Health and Medical Insurance Carriers, despite the fact that a number are registered in the CCR. There may be valid reasons for this. This may be an industry that SBA needs to remove from the calculation of goaling dollars because of the infeasibility of using small businesses. Alternatively, the small-business threshold for this industry may need to be increased significantly by SBA in response to economies of scale and industry consolidation. The low number of contracts and purchase offices used to buy goods and services in this industry may also indicate that strategic sourcing has already leveraged purchases in this industry as much as is feasibly possible. Regardless, policymakers should consider whether small-business

---

[1]   The CCR is the primary vendor-registrant database for the federal government. It collects, validates, stores, and disseminates basic vendor data in support of federal government requirements. All DoD vendors must register in this system to be awarded a contract. Hence, it determines the size of the marketplace from which DoD can purchase goods and services. Firms may register in multiple industries; indeed, some firms in the CCR are registered in nearly 1,000 industries. Firms may be small for some industry classifications but other-than-small for others.

Although the CCR indicates that relatively large proportions of vendors in each of these industries are small businesses, the specific goods and services offered by these small businesses varies greatly by industry and hence constrains DoD ability to select small businesses for some goods and services more than may immediately be apparent. We will discuss this below when we assess DoD's expenditures with small business by industry and budget category.

Table 3.3
Leading Industries for DoD Operations and Maintenance Purchases, FY 2012

NAICS Code	Industry Name	Goaling Dollars (millions)	% of Small-Business	No. of Contracts[a]	No. of Purchase Offices[b]	Small-Business Threshold (Annual Receipts in Dollars or No. of Employees in Firm)	No. of CCR Contractors	% of Small-Business CCR Contractors
541330	Engineering Services	14,666	15	4,871	474	$14.0M to $37.5M	39,932	64
324110	Petroleum Refineries	11,531	12	804	52	1,500 workers	590	62
524114	Direct Health and Medical Insurance Carriers	10,029	0	11	10	$7.0M	468	42
336413	Other Aircraft Parts and Auxiliary Equipment Manufacturing	5,860	12	21,277	369	1,000 workers	4,868	79
336411	Aircraft Manufacturing	5,147	7	2,295	195	1,500 workers	2,030	75
236220	Commercial and Institutional Building Construction	4,601	69	3,627	254	$33.5M	31,586	80
336611	Ship Building and Repairing	4,021	18	1,632	90	1,000 workers	1,807	79
541519	Other Computer Related Services	3,954	39	2,823	428	$25.5M	23,779	82
561210	Facilities Support Services	3,617	45	1,137	303	$35.5M	14,667	71
488190	Other Support Activities for Air Transportation	3,377	4	237	114	$30.0M	2,806	65
	Others	70,862	36	288,662	1,096	n/a	n/a	n/a
	Total for all industries	137,665		327,255	1,127			
	Average across all industries		27			n/a	n/a	n/a

SOURCE: FY 2012 FPDS data for goaling dollars.

[a] Written and used by DoD. Because a small number of contracts are used to purchase goods and services in more than one industry, the sum of the number of contracts by industry may exceed the total number of contracts. Our number of "contracts" reflects the number of contracts with unique contract numbers and do not include, as separate contracts, task orders against multiple-award contracts.

[b] Because a purchasing office may purchase goods and services in more than one industry, the sum of purchasing offices by industry can exceed the total number of purchasing offices.

thresholds in this industry, and requirements that DoD use small businesses in this industry, reflect economic reality.

Second, Aircraft Manufacturing appears to be more relevant for Procurement, and not O&M. Nevertheless, large contractor-logistics support contracts are funded from O&M funds and are coded in the FPDS as purchases in the Aircraft Manufacturing industry. We will explore this further in the next chapter.

Third, Ship Building and Repairing combines both manufacturing, which fits in the procurement budget category, and repairing, which fits in the O&M category. This industry definition may be too broad and need to be split into two different industries. This, in turn, would have implications for what is, or is not, a small business engaged in shipbuilding or repairing.

The numbers of contracts and purchase offices used in these industries may also be worth exploring further, in particular to see whether there are needs within these industries that multiple purchase offices are purchasing. Should multiple purchase offices be purchasing common or identical goods and services, then DoD may wish to explore ways to consolidate and leverage these purchases. The high ratio of contracts to purchase offices also may suggest some consolidation possibilities—although any such analysis must consider the number of suppliers holding these contracts as well. In the next chapter, we explore what contract-action data on contractors, purchase offices, and industries may indicate for both small-business and strategic-sourcing initiatives.

CHAPTER FOUR

Identifying Specific Opportunities for Strategic Sourcing and Implications for Small-Business Procurement

The contract-action data we have examined provide not just a general overview of small-business purchases by DoD but also some specific prospective opportunities, and limits, for strategic-sourcing efforts among small businesses. We consider data for specific suppliers, purchasers, and industries. We caution the reader that the examples we present in this chapter are illustrative. Any efforts to identify best targets of opportunity must take into account practical considerations. Some contracts or requirements may not be good candidates for initiatives we describe. DoD personnel are, ultimately, the best arbiters of what purchases and initiatives can best fulfill all DoD needs.

In FY 2012, DoD purchased goods and services through nearly 366,000 unique contracts it had written or used.[1] Examining the number of these contracts by supplier and purchase office can offer some insight on strategic-sourcing opportunities. In particular, consolidating these contracts by supplier or buyer within DoD can help reduce DoD contracting costs, increase DoD leverage or buying power, and thereby help DoD accomplish more with less, as it seeks to do in its strategic-sourcing initiatives.

As ranked by number of contracts, ten contractors have more than 1,350 contracts written and used by DoD, with two contractors each having more than 2,000 such contracts (Table 4.1). One of these, Kampi Components, Inc., has more DoD contracts than any other supplier. Two others in the top ten are, like Kampi, small businesses; they are shown in italics in the table.

Kampi is a small distributor of genuine factory replacement spare parts for aerospace, electrical, and hardware products often made by large producers, such as Boeing, United Technologies, and ITT. The fact that it had more contracts with DoD than any other firm indicates that these contracts could be consolidated—and Kampi would still remain a small business. The fact that Kampi largely resells the goods and services of other suppliers to DoD likely indicates that DoD is using third-party resellers to meet its small-business goals rather than dealing directly with manufacturers, which adds handling costs that increase DoD's total costs.

More than 80 DoD purchase offices acquired goods and services from each of these three small businesses. These contractors sell DoD a wide variety of goods and services, each doing so in more than 100 different industries (as represented by NAICS codes) and for goods and services in more than 150 Product and Service Codes (PSCs), a more finely grained indicator

---

[1] Over two-thirds of these contracts were for less than $25,000 and represented less than 1 percent of DoD contract dollars.

Table 4.1
DoD Contractors Ranked by Number of Contracts, FY 2012

Contractor	No. of Contracts[a]	% of Sole-Source Contracts	Goaling Dollars (millions)	% of Sole-Source Dollars	No. of Purchase Offices	No. of PSCs	No. of Industries
Kampi Components Co., Inc.	*3,282*	*4*	*50*	*6*	*112*	*224*	*177*
BAE Systems, PLC	2,032	26	5,228	38	280	308	163
SAIC, Inc.	1,872	13	4,918	16	312	305	143
Lockheed Martin Corporation	1,809	59	23,394	64	336	389	144
L-3 Communications Holdings, Inc.	1,726	37	5,789	42	291	318	142
General Dynamics Corporation	1,659	40	12,170	61	347	343	160
Martin Military, Inc.	*1,470*	*2*	*28*	*1*	*80*	*172*	*120*
Raytheon Company	1,403	53	10,636	62	208	272	115
Oshkosh Corporation	1,381	8	1,513	20	107	132	90
Pioneer Industries, Inc.	*1,351*	*4*	*30*	*8*	*81*	*154*	*127*
Other contractors	347,969	17	216,746	34	1,131	2,199	1,088
Total for all contractors	365,943		280,501		1,142	2,204	1,089
Average for all contractors		17		39			

SOURCE: FY 2012 FPDS data.

NOTE: Small businesses are shown in italics.

[a] Because a small number of contracts are used to purchase goods and services from more than one parent firm, the sum of the number of contracts by contractor may exceed the total number of contracts. We remind the reader that our number of "contracts" reflects the number of contracts with unique contract numbers and does not include as separate contracts task orders against multiple-award contracts. Similarly, because a purchase office may purchase goods and services from more than one contractor, and multiple contractors may sell goods and services in the same PSC or industry, the total numbers of purchase offices, PSCs, and industries shown are less than their sum.

of goods and services than industry codes.[2] Very few of these goods and services are on sole-source contracts.[3] Consolidating these competitive contracts or requirements could increase DoD leverage with these small-business suppliers and reduce workload for the suppliers and DoD contracting offices[4] while still working to meet DoD small-business goals. At the same time, far greater strategic-sourcing opportunities may be available with other-than-small con-

---

[2]   The greater precision of PSCs helps illustrate some possible imprecision in industry codes. For example, in FY 2012, contracts for the Engineering Services industry (NAICS code 541330) had 653 PSCs associated with it, and contracts for Engineering and Technical Services (PSC R425) had 149 industries associated with it. Similarly, contracts for the Facilities Support Services industry (NAICS code 561210) had 406 PSCs associated with it, and contracts for Facilities Operations Support Services (PSC S216) had 127 industries associated with it.

[3]   Businesses, including small businesses, may gain sole-source contracts for many reasons. Among these reasons are production of a unique product, development of an innovative process, or designation as an exclusive distributor. Policy preferences may also lead to small businesses being designated as sole sources (see, for example, Moore, Cox, et al., 2012).

[4]   Strategic sourcing has initial workload associated with aggregating requirements, performing market research, determining the best way to consolidate requirements to reduce total costs, and identifying the terms and conditions that will attract the best suppliers. This upfront workload is balanced with future workload savings from developing fewer, longer-term contracts. See Moore, Grammich, and Bickel (2007) for more on this process.

tractors with high numbers of contracts, through which DoD spends billions for an even wider variety of goods and services.

Multiple contracts for the same commodity may also offer some strategic-sourcing opportunities through contract consolidation as well.[5] DoD uses at least 4,200 contracts for goods and services in ten PSCs (Table 4.2). In most of these, the percentage of dollars spent on sole-source contracts exceeds the percentage of contracts that are sole source, indicating that some sole-source contract consolidation has likely taken place. Nevertheless, for all of these, the number of contracts exceeds the number of parent firms. In six PSCs, the number of contracts was five times the number of parent firms; in two, it was ten times the number of parent firms. This indicates that there may be some opportunity for consolidation of purchases of similar goods and services from the same supplier, leveraging DoD spend.

Table 4.2
DoD PSCs Ranked by Number of Contracts, FY 2012

PSC	No. of Contracts	% of Sole-Source Contracts	Goaling Dollars (millions)	% of Sole-Source Dollars	No. of Purchase Offices	No. of Parent Firms	% of Dollars to Small Businesses
Medical and Surgical Instruments, Equipment, and Supplies	10,311	44	965	15	261	1,695	22
Airframe Structural Components	9,262	8	5,472	83	161	888	4
Hardware, Commercial	7,500	15	233	21	326	1,821	59
Valves, Nonpowered	7,403	11	174	28	129	738	64
Automatic Data Processing (ADP) Software	6,780	31	2,298	17	471	2,470	41
Hose, Pipe, Tube, Lubrication, and Railing Fittings	6,199	5	92	12	132	922	62
Support-Professional: Other	4,746	27	6,417	37	435	2,735	24
Switches	4,512	4	87	13	163	657	69
Miscellaneous Aircraft Accessories and Components	4,253	31	4,361	78	258	944	6
Packing and Gasket Materials	4,211	10	87	30	134	788	54
Other PSCs	304,259	17	260,315	38	1,135	50,958	20
Total for all PSCs[a]	365,943		280,501		1,142	53,963	
Average across all PSCs		17		39			20

SOURCE: FY 2012 FPDS data.

[a] Because a small number of contracts are used to purchase goods and services from more than one PSC, the sum of the number of contracts by PSC may exceed the total number of contracts. We remind the reader that our number of "contracts" reflects the number of contracts with unique contract numbers and does not include as separate contracts task orders against multiple-award contracts. Similarly, because a purchase office may purchase goods and services in multiple PSCs, and parent firms may sell goods and services in more than one PSC, the total numbers of purchase offices and parent firms shown are less than their sum.

---

[5]   For more on consolidating requirements, see Baldwin, Camm, and Moore (2001).

Many of these suppliers are small businesses. For the five PSCs shown, DoD spent more than 50 percent with small businesses. Possibly promising PSCs for strategic sourcing with small business include purchases for Switches and for Hose, Pipe, Tube, Lubrication, and Railing Fittings. For both of these PSCs, DoD has fewer than 200 purchase offices and spends more than 60 percent with small businesses through a number of contracts that is nearly seven times the number of parent firms. Consolidating contracts with some small businesses selling these goods, or otherwise establishing opportunities for preferred small-business suppliers, might offer some opportunities for strategic-sourcing initiatives.[6] At the same time, other opportunities will also be needed to meet strategic-sourcing goals, given the relatively small amount of money DoD spends for these particular goods. We will return to this point in discussing the conclusions and implications of this research.

Multiple purchasers of the same commodity may offer still further strategic-sourcing opportunities (Table 4.3). More than 340 purchase offices buy goods and services from each of ten different PSCs, indicating how widely used these goods and services are. Nevertheless, there may be opportunities for contract consolidation and strategic sourcing across these multiple purchase offices.

For all these PSCs, the number of contracts is at least three times the number of purchase offices buying these goods and services; for five of them, the number of contracts is seven times greater than the number of purchase offices. This likely indicates that purchase offices are using multiple contracts to buy similar goods and services. Although it may be necessary to purchase from multiple suppliers, the number of contracts also exceeds the number of suppliers and is twice the number of suppliers in six of these PSCs. In half of these PSCs, the proportion of contracts that are sole source is greater than the percentage of dollars spent on sole-source contracts, possibly indicating some sole-source consolidation opportunities as well.

Many of the purchases for these common items acquired across purchase offices are with small businesses. Altogether, for goods and services in five of these PSCs, DoD spent at least 40 percent of its dollars with small businesses. For two of these PSCs, Miscellaneous Alarm, Signal, and Security Detection Systems, and Office Furniture, DoD spent at least 60 percent of its dollars with small businesses. The number of DoD contracts for these PSCs are three to four times greater than the number of purchase offices acquiring such goods and about twice the number of parent firms from which DoD purchases these goods. Establishing some preferred small-business suppliers and consolidating contracts with them up to the small-business threshold for their industries could help meet strategic-sourcing goals and reduce demands on contract staff.

Establishing umbrella contracts for preferred small-business suppliers of office furniture might offer multiple ways to implement strategic sourcing. The federal government has long sought to channel purchases to UNICOR, traditionally one of the leading producers of office furniture for the federal government; currently DoD is required to purchase from UNICOR in industries where it has less than a 5 percent market share (Moore et al., 2004; Chacko, 2012). To the extent that UNICOR falls below a 5 percent market share in office-furniture industries and DoD purchase offices buy office furniture from other sources, DoD may wish to explore how small businesses providing these goods can better fulfill its needs and establish appropriate umbrella relationships.

---

[6]   For more on this point, see, in addition to Baldwin, Camm, and Moore (2001), Moore et al. (2002), and Moore, Grammich, and Bickel (2007).

Table 4.3
DoD PSCs Ranked by Number of Purchase Offices, FY 2012

PSC	No. of Purchase Offices	No. of Contracts	% of Sole-Source Contracts	Goaling Dollars (millions)	% of Sole-Source Dollars	No. of Parent Firms	% of Dollars to Small Businesses
ADP Software	471	6,780	31	2,298	17	2,470	41
Office Furniture	467	1,896	11	341	11	892	60
Miscellaneous Communications Equipment	466	3,463	33	2,919	54	1,398	23
Support-Professional: Engineering/Technical	436	3,541	34	14,766	24	1,511	21
Support-Professional: Other	435	4,746	27	6,417	37	2,735	24
ADP Support Equipment	422	2,424	15	674	8	1,218	47
ADP Input/Output and Storage Devices	414	2,064	247	396	21	909	42
ADP Equipment System Configuration	355	1,315	18	858	8	683	38
Miscellaneous Alarm, Signal, and Security Detection Systems	346	1,086	22	178	43	580	61
Miscellaneous Electrical and Electronic Components	343	2,733	17	678	57	1,191	19
Other PSCs	1,137	341,460	16	250,977	40	50,920	19
Total for all PSCs[a]	1,142	365,943		280,501		53,963	
Average across all PSCs			17		39		20

SOURCE: FY 2012 FPDS data.

[a] Because purchase offices may purchase goods and services in more than one PSC, the total number of purchase offices is less than the sum of them by PSC. Similarly, because a small number of contracts are used to purchase goods and services from more than one PSC, the sum of the number of contracts by PSC may exceed the total number of contracts. We remind the reader that our number of "contracts" reflects the number of contracts with unique contract numbers and do not include as separate contracts task orders against multiple-award contracts. Finally, because parent firms may sell goods and services in more than one PSC, the total shown is less than their sum by PSC.

Another way to identify prospective strategic-sourcing opportunities is to identify areas where DoD spends a large amount of money and has a large number of contracts used by a large number of purchase offices. As we have seen, large numbers of contracts are one indicator of a strategic-sourcing opportunity, particularly in contract consolidation. Large numbers of purchase offices are another, particularly to the extent that DoD can consolidate purchases with many buyers and thereby leverage its total overall spend. High levels of spending, although perhaps less relevant to small businesses, are still another opportunity, with DoD likely to realize the most savings in areas where it spends the most money.

Table 4.4 ranks, by total amount DoD spends in them, industries that are in the top 50 for DoD goaling dollars and number of contracts and number of purchase offices buying goods and services in the industry. DoD purchases from small businesses exceed 20 percent

Table 4.4
Industries Among Top 50 for DoD Goaling Dollars, Contracts, and Purchase Offices

NAICS Code	Industry Name	Goaling Dollars (millions)	Goaling Dollars as a % of DoD Total	No. of Contracts[a]	No. of Purchase Offices[b]	Small-Business Threshold (Annual Receipts in Dollars or No. of Employees in Firm)	% of Dollars to Small Businesses
541330	Engineering Services	26,399	9.4	6,457	513	$14.0–$35.5M	15
236220	Commercial and Institutional Building Construction	12,495	4.5	5,100	267	$33.5M	52
336413	Other Aircraft Parts and Auxiliary Equipment Manufacturing	10,368	3.7	21,724	398	1,000	9
334511	Search, Detection, Navigation, Guidance, Aeronautical, and Nautical System and Instrument Manufacturing	7,168	2.6	3,975	383	750	5
336992	Military Armored Vehicle, Tank, and Tank Component Manufacturing	5,772	2.1	2,317	262	1,000	3
541519	Other Computer Related Services	4,575	1.6	3,102	471	$25.5M	39
334220	Radio and Television Broadcasting and Wireless Communications Equipment Manufacturing	4,036	1.4	4,711	452	750	18
541611	Administrative Management and General Management Consulting Services	3,173	1.1	1,952	391	$14.0M	24
541511	Custom Computer Programing Services	2,992	1.1	2,363	418	$25.5M	28
334111	Electronic Computer Manufacturing	1,716	0.6	2,260	495	1,000	35
334419	Other Electronic Component Manufacturing	1,633	0.6	7,209	300	500	9
334290	Other Communications Equipment Manufacturing	1,400	0.5	2,037	474	750	20
333319	Other Commercial and Service Industry Machinery Manufacturing	1,169	0.4	1,911	345	1,000	24
511210	Software Publishing	633	0.2	3,851	408	$35.5M	30
	Total for all industries	280,501	100	365,943	1,142		
	Average across all industries					n/a	20

SOURCE: FY 2012 FPDS data.

[a] We remind the reader that our number of "contracts" reflects the number of contracts with unique contract numbers and does not include as separate contracts task orders against multiple-award contracts.

[b] Because purchase offices may purchase goods and services from more than one industry, the total number of purchase offices for all industries will exceed the sum of purchase offices buying goods and services in each industry.

(or, for that matter, the 23 percent government-wide goal for small-business purchases) in six of these and are 35 percent or higher in three of these.

Yet, DoD small-business purchases remain quite low in several industries and are below 10 percent in four of them. There may be valid reasons why the rate of contracting with small businesses is low in some industries. This may indicate the need to develop sole sources with original-equipment manufacturers to support large weapon systems. Although consolidating contracts with large, sole-source firms does not increase small-business contracting, it can meet strategic-sourcing goals. And, indeed, as we saw above, to meet strategic-sourcing goals, DoD may have to target industries where it purchases the most goods and services—and where small businesses are less prevalent.

A further reason why small businesses may be less prevalent in industries where DoD has the largest and most widespread purchases is the concentration in these industries—presumably leading to an increase in the minimum size an individual firm needs to compete in such industries. Table 4.5 shows, for the industries that are in the top 50 for DoD goaling dollars and number of contracts and number of purchase offices buying goods and services in the industry, the total number of firms and the number of firms that have more than 5,000 employees or more than $100 million in annual receipts. In all these industries, a small proportion of firms are responsible for a much larger proportion of industry revenue. In 11, fewer than 10 percent of firms are responsible for at least 40 percent of revenue. In three of these industries, fewer than 20 firms are responsible for at least 80 percent of revenue. These data indicate some highly consolidated industries. The more consolidated an industry, the larger a business in it must be to be competitive. The a larger a business must be to compete, the higher the small-business size threshold should be in its industry.

Table 4.5
Industries Among Top 50 for DoD Goaling Dollars, Contracts, and Purchase Offices: Number of Firms and Activity for Large Firms

NAICS Code	Industry Name	Total No. of Firms	Large Firms (More Than $100 Million in Annual Receipts or 5,000 Employees)	Large Firms (% of Total Industry Firms)	Large Firms (% of Total Industry Revenue)
541330	Engineering Services	47,714	541	1.1	55.0
236220	Commercial and Institutional Building Construction	36,909	553	1.5	46.6
336413	Other Aircraft Parts and Auxiliary Equipment Manufacturing	770	27	3.5	70.5
334511	Search, Detection, Navigation, Guidance, Aeronautical, and Nautical System and Instrument Manufacturing	494	19	3.8	80.8
336992	Military Armored Vehicle, Tank, and Tank Component Manufacturing	61	5	8.2	80.9
541519	Other Computer Related Services	10,526	98	0.9	45.8
334220	Radio and Television Broadcasting and Wireless Communications Equipment Manufacturing	844	27	3.2	67.6
541611	Administrative Management and General Management Consulting Services	59,612	281	0.5	41.3
541511	Custom Computer Programming Services	52,764	345	0.7	31.3
334111	Electronic Computer Manufacturing	413	14	3.4	87.5
334419	Other Electronic Component Manufacturing	1,289	26	2.0	22.2
334290	Other Communications Equipment Manufacturing	427	13	3.0	48.2
333319	Other Commercial and Service Industry Machinery Manufacturing	1,174	19	1.6	18.8
511210	Software Publishing	5,917	259	4.4	82.4

SOURCES: FY 2012 FPDS data; U.S. Census Bureau (undated-b).

CHAPTER FIVE

Conclusions and Recommendations: Improving the Classification of Small Businesses and Adjusting to Changing DoD Needs

Improving the Classification of Small Businesses

DoD purchases goods and services from many industries, but the share that small businesses have of the federal marketplace differs from what they have in the overall industry. Although there may be many reasons for this, industry-size standards contribute to the disparity. Even at the level of the six-digit NAICS code, industries can be very broad and can include many activities outside DoD requirements and likely undertaken by smaller firms than those that can fulfill its requirements.

Changing economic conditions over time have also affected the thresholds. There is some evidence that economic activity is more concentrated among larger firms—that is, those with at least 500 employees—in recent years than it was in the past. Yet, for most manufacturing industries, the anchor-size threshold remains at 500 employees. SBA has adjusted thresholds over time for receipt-based industries but, historically, these have not kept pace with inflation let alone with industry consolidation.

Data issues also indicate some problems with current thresholds and their effectiveness in identifying small businesses. In some industries, contract-action data indicate that DoD purchases alone exceed the reported size of the industry in the Economic Census. This raises questions about the actual characteristics of industries and how to determine small size within them.

Such issues matter for strategic sourcing because, although the federal government has long sought to boost small business, in setting small-business procurement preferences it has also sought to boost those businesses of sufficient size to handle federal contracting. From this, we infer that small businesses, properly defined, can help boost strategic-sourcing efforts as well. Put another way, strategic sourcing in the commercial sector has already led to stronger, larger businesses, reshaping the characteristics of given industries and the distribution of firms by size within them. In such case, policymakers may need to reconsider exactly what a "small" business is within a given industry.

So, how might small businesses be defined in such a way as to both boost small businesses and serve DoD's strategic-sourcing efforts? We propose several ideas, involving both individual firm characteristics as well as the size distribution of firms within an industry.

A central goal of small-business programs is to "maintain the vigor of the competitive system" (U.S. House of Representatives Select Committee on Small Business, 1952). Competitive markets are typically thought of as markets with a substantial number of suppliers, in which production is not dominated by a few leading firms and in which it is easy for firms to enter and exit. Because the average cost of production usually falls as the production level increases, firms in many cases must achieve a minimum level of production to survive. The size threshold for a small business might be based in part on the minimum size required to be an ongoing concern in the industry. Having small-business size thresholds better reflect market realities would also help balance small-business purchasing goals against other DoD purchasing goals, such as those of strategic sourcing.

SBA should review production processes to determine the minimum size needed for the firm to remain competitive in an industry. The size of firms when they are born and die may help determine what size is needed to remain competitive, although this would be only a broad guideline.[1] The size needed to remain competitive may be greater than that of new entrants because new firms may expect to lose money during a startup period. It also may be above the level of production at which average cost is minimized because firms could survive over the long run at lower production levels.

Access to credit on favorable terms is also critical to a firm's ability to enter the market, finance ongoing operations, and expand. SBA selected its initial $1 million size threshold for service industries in part because it was "viewed as sufficient in addressing the problems of access to credit by small business" (SBA, 2009, p. 7). The $1 million threshold has increased over the years to account for inflation, but there does not appear to have been a "ground-up" reassessment of whether the threshold is appropriate.

SBA could base an industry's size threshold in part on the size needed for the firm to access credit on reasonable terms. Determining this size could be based on review of the credit terms available to firms of different sizes in the industry and discussions with firms, banks, and SBA lending staff. Judgment would be required to assess the point at which the credit terms relative to those available to the largest firms in the industry are cause for concern.

The Small Business Act seeks to "insure that a fair proportion of the total purchases . . . for the [federal] government . . . be placed with small business[es]" (Public Law 85-536, 2013). To succeed in securing government business, firms must, as noted, be of sufficient size to compete for and administer federal prime contracts. It thus seems reasonable to base size thresholds at least in part on the size needed to support the administrative and reporting requirements of prime federal contracts.

Such an assessment could start with estimates of the number of staff needed to administer the types of contracts typically issued by the federal government in a particular industry. The number of production employees or level of output necessary to fund these personnel while keeping overhead rates at a reasonable level could then be determined.

In addition to considering characteristics of individual firms, criteria for setting small-business thresholds should also consider characteristics of an industry, including distribution of firms in concentrated industries. Such criteria could further promote competitiveness. Implementing such criteria would require a census of firms by industry that disaggregates broad industries as appropriate and identifies firms that operate in multiple industries.

A common measure of industry concentration is the Herfindahl-Hirshman Index (HHI).[2] The U.S. Department of Justice and the Federal Trade Commission use the HHI in

---

[1] Statistics of U.S. Businesses (U.S. Census Bureau, 2013) include data on establishment "births" and "deaths" by employment size for industries as defined by four-digit NAICS codes.

[2] The HHI is the sum of the squared market shares for all firms in the industry. A firm's market share is (firm receipts × 100) / total industry receipts.

deciding whether to approve mergers and acquisitions. The cutoffs used to characterize industry concentration are

- less than 1,500:   not concentrated
- 1,500 to 2,500:   moderately concentrated
- more than 2,500: highly concentrated (U.S. Department of Justice and Federal Trade Commission, 2010).

Authorities are more vigilant about mergers when the HHI exceeds 2,500. In such industries, policymakers may wish to identify the leading firms and set the size threshold just below the size of the smallest leading firm.[3] Leading firms might be identified by ranking them by their market shares and noting those with substantial market shares (e.g., more than 10 percent). This approach could result in a much higher size threshold than warranted by measures based on firm characteristics. Such a higher threshold would be justified by the urgent need to promote competitiveness in the industry.

The size standards derived from each of the above criteria will likely differ, meaning that a rule on how to weight them for one standard would need to be developed. All the criteria proposed are critical to achieving one or more of the small-business program goals, so it is appropriate to set the size standard at a level at which all are satisfied and all firms eligible for small-business size preferences are viable. In other words, satisfying all criteria may mean satisfying the largest size standard indicated by the adopted criteria and not an average of the standards. This would mean that the size standard would be set so that a firm would be large enough to be an ongoing concern in the industry, able to access credit on reasonable terms, able to compete for and administer federal prime contracts, and just below the size of the smallest leading firm.

Such adjustment to size standards could appear to reduce competition by reducing opportunities for smaller firms that might face greater competition from larger firms falling below "small" size thresholds. Yet, adjusting small-business size thresholds to reflect what is truly needed to compete for federal and DoD contracts would provide firms, policymakers, and contracting officers a truer perspective of the marketplace for an industry, the capable producers within it, and what is required to remain successful. Furthermore, if federal size thresholds are too low, small firms may not be able to compete in the commercial sector and may become dependent on federal revenue. This would place them at high risk of failure should federal expenditures shrink significantly.

A process for determining appropriate small-business size thresholds for procurement purposes, one that both boosts competitiveness and recognizes the requirements of federal agencies, might first consider legislative definitions and requirements (Figure 5.1). The second step would consider whether the industry is homogeneous in firm size and spending between subindustries. If it is not, then DoD may wish to work with policymakers to derive more homogeneous industries for classification. The third step would consider whether the measure used for the industry—employees, receipts, or still other—is appropriate. If it is not, then the industry measure should change to reflect new operational realities. For homogeneous

---

[3]   An industry comprising ten firms, each with a 10 percent market share, would have an HHI of 1,000 and, by Federal Trade Commission standards, be on the border between industries considered not to be concentrated and those considered to be moderately concentrated. A 10 percent market share might be considered a plausible starting point for considering the appropriate size cutoff for a highly concentrated industry.

Figure 5.1
Overview of a Proposed Size Standard Methodology

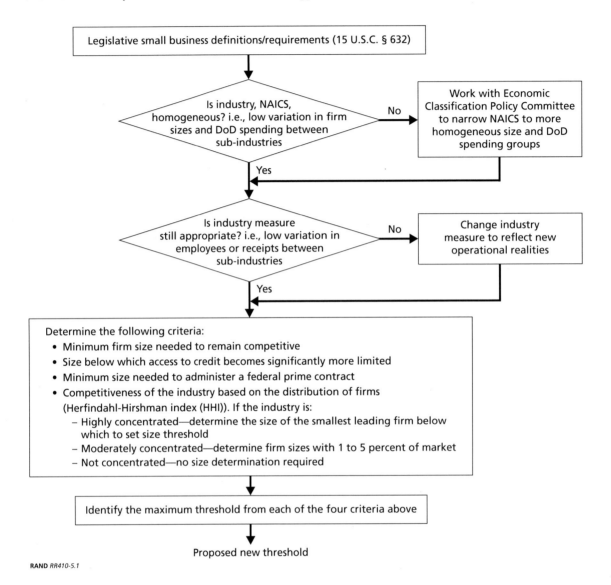

RAND *RR410-5.1*

industries with appropriate measures, policymakers should consider (1) the minimum firm size needed to remain competitive, (2) the firm size sufficient to attract credit, (3) the minimum size needed to administer a federal prime contract, and (4) the competitiveness of the industry, selecting the maximum firm size that will satisfy all these criteria.

In summary, better and more focused definitions might help to set small-business size thresholds for procurement purposes—and to identify small businesses that can both help boost competitiveness and be of sufficient size to help DoD meet its strategic-sourcing goals. This could include determining if industries are defined properly for purposes of setting small-business size thresholds and how firm activity in an industry might best be measured. Consideration of the anchor thresholds, particularly in light of procurement requirements, might help as well; there appears to be no justification for current standards but historical precedent. Conditions in some industries may have changed sufficiently that they now require a differing measure, e.g., number of employees rather than average annual receipts, to determine what is a small firm. Regardless of method chosen, any new method should consider the minimum firm size needed to stay competitive and perform government work, weighting, as necessary, those characteristics most appropriate for government preferences.

Adjusting to Changing DoD Needs

In reviewing recent DoD spending, we found that in many industries where DoD concentrates its spending, spending is large and small-business revenue thresholds are not keeping pace with inflation or industry consolidations. We also found that DoD spending is very fragmented, with large numbers of contracts across many different firms and contracting offices. We also found many sole-source contracts with DoD suppliers, including both small businesses and some of its largest suppliers.

In coming years, we expect that DoD budget cuts will change its mix of spending, which in turn will affect its small-business utilization and its strategic-sourcing opportunities. DoD has spent a great deal with small businesses that provide Operations and Maintenance, but funding for this category will decrease in coming years. DoD will therefore need to increase its utilization of small businesses in this or other categories to meet its small-business goals. To do this, it needs to carefully analyze its spending and small-business use and find areas where increasing spending with small businesses is most feasible. It also needs to assess the reasonableness of current SBA industry thresholds and the availability of willing small firms with the right capabilities to meet its requirements, and it may need to actively work to get them changed.

Similarly, we conclude that proposed budget cuts are likely to occur largely in industries where DoD already has a high rate of contracting with small businesses and may need to further increase it. We also note that industries that have consolidated or are consolidating provide particular challenges. To meet its future small-business goals, DoD may need to press to revise industry

- thresholds, to reflect not only inflation but also industry consolidation
- metrics, such as high inputs to production, to reflect the realities of certain industry operations, and
- definitions, to reflect the demographics of industries as well as new and emerging technologies that do not fit the current definitions.

Strategic sourcing could benefit some small firms by providing them with fewer, larger, longer-term contracts. Yet, such opportunities are limited by current industry definitions and SBA size policies.

To ensure that its goals for small-business utilization and strategic sourcing do not conflict, we recommend that DoD identify the industries where it has opportunities to increase its contracting with small-business–utilization rate through strategic sourcing. We further recommend that DoD consider developing a small-business preferred-supplier program for those small businesses that have demonstrated good performance and value. Such a program might build on efforts of the Better Buying Power initiative to extend the Navy's Preferred Supplier Program to a DoD-wide pilot. This initiative would "recognize and reward businesses and corporations that consistently demonstrate exemplary performance" (Carter, 2010). In particular, the Navy has sought to allow contracting authorities to set favorable terms and conditions, recognizing firms that demonstrate superior performance in delivering goods and services.

DoD may wish to strongly advocate raising small-business thresholds where industries are highly consolidated or are consolidating as well as where thresholds have not kept pace with inflation. It may also wish to work with policymakers to improve and expedite the SBA's process for determining thresholds and to validate or change industry metrics that do not adequately reflect the realities of doing business. Finally, it may want to work with the Office of Management and Budget to refine industry (NAICS) definitions to better reflect industry demographics as well as emerging technologies.

In pursuing both strategic-sourcing and small-business initiatives, DoD will continually face tensions between the two. Small-business goals seek, in part, to increase the number of firms participating in federal government contracts. Strategic sourcing, by contrast, would lead to more requirements being met by fewer firms but with the risk that small firms that receive fewer but larger contracts grow to the extent that they exceed the size threshold for their industry—and reduce overall DoD purchases from small business. Given the charge to pursue both small-business policies and strategic-sourcing initiatives, DoD policymakers may understandably seek to apply strategic sourcing to their contracts with small businesses. This document shows some ways that they can do so. Yet the tension between the two will remain.

Overview of Data Used in the Analyses

In this appendix, we provide an overview of the data we used for some of the analyses in this document, particularly firm-level Economic Census data and Federal Procurement Data System data.

Economic Census Data

The Census Bureau collects data on U.S. businesses every five years, obtaining information about establishments and firms, employment, labor costs, expenses, sales, assets, inventories, and capital expenditures in their predominant industry. The most recently available data are from 2007. Previous Economic Censuses using the North American Industry Classification System were conducted in 2002 and 1997. Results from the 2012 Economic Census will be available in coming years.

Publicly available Economic Census data about firms are aggregated into cells, defined by industry code and size measured primarily using employment or sales. For confidentiality reasons, Economic Census data are not provided when only one or a few firms or establishments are in a cell or cells, such that particular firms could be identified. Such industries with suppressed data include Ammunition (Except Small Arms) Manufacturing (NAICS code 332993) and Military Armored Vehicle, Tank, and Tank Component Manufacturing (NAICS code 336992. Reardon and Moore (2005) tested a number of methods for estimating missing data and found that approximating these from higher-level NAICS codes provides a reasonable estimation.

Federal Procurement Data System Data

Many of our analyses of DoD expenditures are based on contract-action data available in the Federal Procurement Data System. A contract action is generated when a contracting officer signs a document related to a contract initiation or award, when contracts are modified (e.g., obligations, deobligations, option-year awards, administrative changes that alter contract language in any way), when contract orders or payments are made using a government purchase card, or when contracts are terminated.

Contract actions (reported singly or in aggregate) above the micro-purchase threshold, which is currently set at $3,000, must be reported to the FPDS including, among other variables, the name and address of the contractor, contractor and industry identification codes,

NAICS code of the contractor, the Federal Supply Class or PSC of the goods or services purchased, whether the contractor is a small business, and, if so, whether it is eligible for certain preferences.

We analyze contracts from which goods or services are ultimately purchased. Our number of "contracts" reflects the number of contracts with unique contract-numbers, and do not include as separate contracts task orders against multiple-award contracts.

Our analyses are of "goaling" dollars, a subset of all contract dollars that are considered when determining whether an agency and the federal government met its small-business procurement goals. Goaling dollars exclude

- contracts performed outside the United States
- acquisitions by agencies on behalf of foreign governments or entities or international organizations
- contracts funded predominantly with agency-generated sources
- purchases made under the Javits-Wagner-O'Day (Sheltered Workshop) Program
- purchases from UNICOR
- purchases from the American Institute in Taiwan
- purchases for TRICARE (the health care program serving Uniformed Service members, retirees, and their families worldwide).

The Federal Funding Accountability and Transparency Act of 2006 requires that the Treasury Account Symbol (TAS) be included as a part of the data on contract actions reported to the FPDS that have nonzero dollar amounts. These data help to provide insight into the use of taxpayer dollars by identifying which types of appropriations are used on contracts. The TAS is made up of three data elements: a two-character agency identifier, a four-character main account code, and a three-character subaccount code. It is usually available in the line of accounting that customers provide in the funding part of their requirements documents. The agency identifier identifies the organization, such as a military service or the Defense Logistics Agency. The main account code identifies the type of fund and the purpose of the account within that fund, such as the type of appropriation. The subaccount code identifies a subdivision of the main account. TAS codes are assigned by the Department of Treasury and are managed by federal organizations. The type of appropriation, such as Operations and Maintenance or Military Construction, is discernible through TAS agency and main account codes and can be identified from publications or guides from the Department of Treasury, Office of Management and Budget, or DoD. We used these sources to link contract actions to budget categories for determining the percentage use of small businesses by budget category.

DoD does some buying for non-DoD agencies using non-DoD funds. We did not include these contract actions when determining and projecting small business spending by budget category.

Our industry analyses were, as indicated, based on NAICS codes reported on the contract-action reports.

References

13 CFR §121, Small Business Size Regulations, annual.

A. T. Kearney, Inc., "Merger Endgames: Industry Consolidation and Long-Term Strategy," Chicago, Ill., 2001.

"Aid for Small Business—The Story of Federal Action," *Congressional Digest*, Vol. 35, No. 12, December 1956, pp. 291–292.

Arena, Mark V., Irv Blickstein, Obaid Younossi, and Clifford A. Grammich, *Why Has the Cost of Navy Ships Risen? A Macroscopic Examination of the Trends in U.S. Naval Ship Costs over the Past Several Decades*, Santa Monica, Calif.: RAND Corporation, MG-484-NAVY, 2006. As of April 3, 2013: http://www.rand.org/pubs/monographs/MG484.html

Baldwin, Laura H., Frank Camm, and Nancy Y. Moore, *Federal Contract Bundling: A Framework for Making and Justifying Decisions for Purchased Services*, Santa Monica, Calif.: RAND Corporation, MR-1224-AF, 2001. As of April 14, 2013: http://www.rand.org/pubs/monograph_reports/MR1224.html

Bean, Jonathan J., *Beyond the Broker State: Federal Policies Toward Small Business, 1936–1961*, Chapel Hill, N.C.: University of North Carolina Press, 1996.

———, *Big Government and Affirmative Action: The Scandalous History of the Small Business Administration*, Lexington, Ky.: University Press of Kentucky, 2001.

Berthoff, Rowland, "Independence and Enterprise: Small Business in the American Dream," in Stuart W. Bruchey, ed., *Small Business in American Life*, Washington, D.C.: Beard Books, [1980], 2003.

Birkler, John, Paul Bracken, Gordon T. Lee, Mark A. Lorell, Soumen Saha, and Shane Tierney, *Keeping a Competitive U.S. Military Aircraft Industry Aloft: Findings from an Analysis of the Industrial Base*, Santa Monica, Calif.: RAND Corporation, MG-1133-OSD, 2011. As of May 2, 2013: http://www.rand.org/pubs/monographs/MG1133.html

Carter, Ashton B., "Memorandum for Acquisition Professionals on Better Buying Power: Guidance for Obtaining Greater Efficiency and Productivity in Defense Spending," September 14, 2010. As of September 16, 2013: http://www.acq.osd.mil/docs/USD_ATL_Guidance_Memo_September_14_2010_FINAL.PDF

Chacko, Sarah, "Critics Target Federal Prison Industries' Contracting Preferences," *Federal Times*, June 29, 2012. As of April 19, 2013: http://www.federaltimes.com/article/20120629/ACQUISITION03/306290007/ Critics-target-Federal-Prison-Industries-8217-contracting-preferences

Chenoweth, Mary E., Jeremy Arkes, and Nancy Y. Moore, *Best Practices in Developing Proactive Supply Strategies for Air Force Low-Demand Service Parts,* Santa Monica, Calif.: RAND Corporation, MG-858-AF, 2010. As of May 2, 2013: http://www.rand.org/pubs/monographs/MG858.html

Chenoweth, Mary E., and Clifford A. Grammich, *The F100 Engine Purchasing and Supply Chain Management Demonstration: Findings from Air Force Spend Analyses*, Santa Monica, Calif.: RAND Corporation, MG-424-AF, 2006. As of April 14, 2013: http://www.rand.org/pubs/monographs/MG424.html

Chenoweth, Mary E., Nancy Y. Moore, Amy G. Cox, Judith D. Mele, and Jerry M. Sollinger, *Best Practices in Supplier Relationship Management and Their Early Implementation in the Air Force Materiel Command*, Santa Monica, Calif.: RAND Corporation, TR-904-AF, 2012. As of April 14, 2013:
http://www.rand.org/pubs/technical_reports/TR904.html

Cox, Amy G., Nancy Y. Moore, and Clifford A. Grammich, *Identifying and Eliminating Barriers Faced by Nontraditional Department of Defense Suppliers*, Santa Monica, Calif.: RAND Corporation RR-267-OSD, forthcoming.

Czech, Peter, and John Mueller, "Improving Services Acquisition Tradecraft," *Defense AT&L*, July–August 2011, pp. 42–46. As of April 30, 2011:
http://www.dau.mil/pubscats/ATL%20Docs/July-Aug11/DATL%20July-Aug11.pdf

Deans, Graeme K., Fritz Kroeger, and Stefan Zeisel, "The Consolidation Curve," *Harvard Business Review*, Vol. 80, No. 12, December 2002, pp. 20–21.

Dilger, Robert Jay, "Small Business Size Standards: A Historical Analysis of Contemporary Issues," Washington, D.C.: Congressional Research Service, December 6, 2012.

Federal Register, "Procurement of Military Supplies and Animals: General Purchase Policies," June 17, 1944.

———, "Title 10, Chapter 8, Part 851," June 9, 1948.

———, "Title 13, Chapter II, Part 103, Small Business Size Standards," December 7, 1956.

———, "Small Business Size Standards: Professional, Technical, and Scientific Services; Final Rule," Vol. 77, No. 28, February 10, 2012, pp. 7490–7514.

Foreman, Tim J., email to Nancy Y. Moore, RAND Corporation, April 9, 2008.

Freedberg, Sydney J., Jr., "2014 Budget: Three Reasons Why Pentagon's Request Is Irrelevant," *Breaking Defense,* April 10, 2013. As of September 15, 2013:
http://breakingdefense.com/2013/04/10/2014-budget-3-reasons-pentagon-request-irrelevant/

Gansler, Jacques S., *Democracy's Arsenal: Creating a Twenty-First-Century Defense Industry,* Cambridge, Mass.: MIT Press, 2011.

Gates, Susan M., and Kristin J. Leuschner, eds., *In the Name of Entrepreneurship? The Logic and Effects of Special Regulatory Treatment for Small Business*, Santa Monica, Calif.: RAND Corporation, MG-663-EMKF, 2007. As of April 14, 2013:
http://www.rand.org/pubs/monographs/MG663.html

General Accounting Office, *Defense Industry Consolidation and Options for Preserving Competition*, 1998. As of April 17, 2013:
http://www.gao.gov/archive/1998/ns98141.pdf

Grammich, Clifford A., Thomas Edison, Nancy Y. Moore, and Edward G. Keating, *Small Business and Defense Acquisitions: An Overview of Policies and Current Practices*, Santa Monica, Calif.: RAND Corporation, MG-443-OSD, 2011. As of February 19, 2013:
http://www.rand.org/pubs/monographs/MG443.html

Gu, Qian, Lynn A. Karoly, and Julie Zissimopoulos, "Small Business Assistance Programs in the United States: An Analysis of What They Are, How Well They Perform, and How We Can Learn More About Them," *International Review of Entrepreneurship*, Vol. 8, No. 3, 2010, pp. 1–32.

Hanks, Christopher, Elliot Axelband, Shuna Lindsay, Mohammed Rehan Malik, and Brett Steele, *Reexamining Military Acquisition Reform: Are We There Yet?* Santa Monica, Calif.: RAND Corporation, MG-291-A, 2005. As of May 28, 2013:
http://www.rand.org/pubs/monographs/MG291.html

Joel Popkin and Company, "Small Business Share of Economic Growth," December 2001. As of March 3, 2013:
http://www.sba.gov/advo/research/rs211tot.pdf

Joel Popkin and Company, "Small Business Share of NAICS Industries," June 2002. As of March 3, 2013:
http://www.sba.gov/advo/research/rs218tot.pdf

Keefe, Ryan, Susan M. Gates, and Eric Talley, "Criteria Used to Define *Small Business* in Determining Thresholds," in Susan M. Gates and Kristin J. Leuschner, eds., *In the Name of Entrepreneurship? The Logic and Effects of Special Regulatory Treatment for Small Business*, Santa Monica, Calif.: RAND Corporation, MG-663-EMKF, 2007. As of March 3, 2013:
http://www.rand.org/pubs/monographs/MG663.html

Kobe, Kathryn, "Small Business GDP: Update 2002–2010," January 2012. As of April 17, 2013:
http://www.sba.gov/sites/default/files/rs390tot_0.pdf

Manuel, Kate M., and Erika K. Lunder, "Federal Contracting and Subcontracting with Small Businesses: Issues in the 112th Congress," Washington, D.C.: Congressional Research Service, January 24, 2013.

Moore, Nancy Y., Laura H. Baldwin, Frank Camm, and Cynthia R. Cook, *Implementing Best Purchasing and Supply Management Practices: Lessons from Innovative Commercial Firms*, Santa Monica, Calif.: RAND Corporation, DB-334-AF, 2002. As of August 12, 2013:
http://www.rand.org/pubs/documented_briefings/DB334.html

Moore, Nancy Y., Mary E. Chenoweth, Elaine Reardon, Clifford A. Grammich, Arthur M. Bullock, Judith D. Mele, Aaron Kofner, and Eric J. Unger, *Estimating DoD Transportation Spending: Analyses of Contract and Payment Transactions*, Santa Monica, Calif.: RAND Corporation, DB-516-TRANSCOM, 2007. As of May 2, 2013:
http://www.rand.org/pubs/documented_briefings/DB516.html

Moore, Nancy Y., Cynthia Cook, Clifford Grammich, and Charles Lindenblatt, *Using a Spend Analysis to Help Identify Prospective Air Force Purchasing and Supply Management Initiatives: Summary of Selected Findings*, Santa Monica, Calif.: RAND Corporation, DB-434-AF, 2004. As of April 19, 2013:
http://www.rand.org/pubs/documented_briefings/DB434.html

Moore, Nancy Y., Amy G. Cox, Clifford A. Grammich, and Judith D. Mele, *Supplier Relationship Management at Army Life Cycle Management Commands: Gap Analysis of Best Practices*, Santa Monica, Calif.: RAND Corporation, DB-608-A, 2012a. As of April 14, 2013:
http://www.rand.org/pubs/documented_briefings/DB608.html

Moore, Nancy Y., Clifford A. Grammich, and Robert Bickel, *Developing Tailored Supply Strategies*, Santa Monica, Calif.: RAND Corporation, MG-572-AF, 2007. As of April 22, 2013:
http://www.rand.org/pubs/monographs/MG572.html

Moore, Nancy Y., Clifford A. Grammich, Mary E. Chenoweth, and Judith D. Mele, *Targets for Marine Corps Purchasing and Supply Management Initiatives: Spend Analysis Findings*, Santa Monica, Calif.: RAND Corporation, DB-512-USMC, 2011. As of May 2, 2013:
http://www.rand.org/pubs/documented_briefings/DB512.html

Moore, Nancy Y., Clifford A. Grammich, Julie DaVanzo, Bruce Held, John Coombs, and Judith D. Mele, *Enhancing Small-Business Opportunities in the DoD*, Santa Monica, Calif.: RAND Corporation, TR-601-1-OSD, 2008. As of February 19, 2013:
http://www.rand.org/pubs/technical_reports/TR601-1.html

Moore, Nancy Y., and Elvira N. Loredo, *Identifying and Managing Air Force Sustainment Supply Chain Risks*, Santa Monica, Calif.: RAND Corporation, DB-649-AF, 2013. As of September 18, 2013:
http://www.rand.org/pubs/documented_briefings/DB649.html

Moore, Nancy Y., Mark Y. D. Wang, Carol E. Fan, and Clifford A. Grammich, *A Gap Analysis of Life Cycle Management Commands and Best Purchasing and Supply Management Organizations*, Santa Monica, Calif.: RAND Corporation, DB-615-A, 2012b. As of May 2, 2013:
http://www.rand.org/pubs/documented_briefings/DB615.html

Nicosia, Nancy, and Nancy Y. Moore, *Implementing Purchasing and Supply Chain Management: Best Practices in Market Research*, Santa Monica, Calif.: RAND Corporation, MG-473-AF, 2006. As of April 14, 2013:
http://www.rand.org/pubs/monographs/MG473.html

Office of Small Business Programs, "Small Business Program Performance History," undated-a. As of April 30, 2013:
http://www.acq.osd.mil/osbp/gov/sbPerformanceHistory.shtml

————, "Small Business Program Goals," undated-b. As of April 18, 2013:
http://www.acq.osd.mil/osbp/gov/sbProgramGoals.shtml

Office of the Under Secretary of Defense (Comptroller), *National Defense Budget Estimates for FY 2013*, March 2012. As of February 14, 2013:
http://comptroller.defense.gov/defbudget/fy2013/FY13_Green_Book.pdf

————, *National Defense Budget Estimates for FY 2014*, May 2013. As of July 13, 2013:
http://comptroller.defense.gov/defbudget/fy2014/FY14_Green_Book.pdf

Public Law 85-536, Small Business Act, as amended through January 3, 2013. As of May 6, 2013:
http://www.sba.gov/content/small-business-act

Reardon, Elaine, and Nancy Y. Moore, *The Department of Defense and Its Use of Small Businesses: An Economic and Industry Analysis*, Santa Monica, Calif.: RAND Corporation, DB-478-OSD, 2005. As of July 2, 2013:
http://www.rand.org/pubs/documented_briefings/DB478.html

Saunders, Kenneth, Bruno Augenstein, Paul Bracken, Glenn Krumel, John Birkler, James Chiesa, Cullen M. Crain, R. Richard Heppe, Richard F. Hoglund, and Brian Nichiporuk, *Priority-Setting and Strategic Sourcing in the Naval Research, Development, and Technology Infrastructure*, Santa Monica, Calif.: RAND Corporation, MR-588-NAVY/OSD, 1995. As of April 14, 2013:
http://www.rand.org/pubs/monograph_reports/MR588.html

SBA—*See* Small Business Administration.

Schank, John F., James G. Kallimani, Jess Chandler, Mark V. Arena, Carter C. Price, and Clifford A. Grammich, *Changing Aircraft Carrier Procurement Schedules: Effects That a Five-Year Procurement Cycle Would Have on Cost, Availability, and Shipyard Manpower and Workload*, Santa Monica, Calif.: RAND Corporation, MG-1073-NAVY, 2011. As of May 2, 2013:
http://www.rand.org/pubs/monographs/MG1073.html

Small Business Administration, "Goaling," undated-a. As of June 29, 2013:
http://www.sba.gov/content/small-business-goaling

————, "Our History," undated-b. As of March 2, 2013:
http://www.sba.gov/about-sba-services/our-history

————, "Small Business Procurement Scorecards," undated-c. As of April 4, 2013:
http://www.sba.gov/content/small-business-procurement-goaling-scorecards

————, "SBA Size Standards Methodology," April 2009. As of March 14, 2013:
http://www.sba.gov/sites/default/files/size_standards_methodology.pdf

————, "Department of Defense, FY 2011 Small Business Procurement Scorecard," 2012. As of April 4, 2013:
http://www.sba.gov/sites/default/files/files/FY11%20Final%20Scorecard%20DOD_2012-06-29.pdf

U.S. Census Bureau, "Statistics About Business Size (Including Small Business)," undated-a. As of April 8, 2013:
http://www.census.gov/econ/smallbus.html

————, "2007 Economic Census," undated-b. As of September 18, 2013:
http://www.census.gov/econ/census07

————, "2007 Economic Census: Methodology," 2009a. As of August 11, 2012:
http://www.census.gov/econ/census07/www/methodology/

————, "2007 Economic Census: Definitions," 2009b. As of July 1, 2013:
http://www.census.gov/econ/census07/www/definitions.html

————, "Statistics of U.S. Businesses," 2013. As of May 3, 2013:
http://www.census.gov/econ/susb/

U.S. Department of Defense, *National Defense Budget Estimates for FY 2013*, March 2012.

U.S. Department of Justice and Federal Trade Commission, "Horizontal Merger Guidelines," August 19, 2010. As of May 7, 2013:
http://www.justice.gov/atr/public/guidelines/hmg-2010.html

U.S. House of Representatives Select Committee on Small Business, "Final Report," 1952.